Easy Chili Cookbook

A Comprehensive Guide To Mouth-Watering, Quick and Delicious Chili Recipes To Prepare At Home For Healthy Eating

Richard Tillcot

© Copyright 2021 Richard Tillcot

All rights reserved.

The content contained within this book may not be reproduced, duplicated or transmitted without direct written permission from the author or the publisher.

Under no circumstances will any blame or legal responsibility be held against the publisher, or author, for any damages, reparation, or monetary loss due to the information contained within this book. Either directly or indirectly.

Legal Notice:

This book is copyright protected. This book is only for personal use. You cannot amend, distribute, sell, use, quote or paraphrase any part, or the content within this book, without the consent of the author or publisher.

Disclaimer Notice:

Please note the information contained within this document is for educational and entertainment purposes only. All effort has been executed to present accurate, up to date, and reliable, complete information. No warranties of any kind are declared or implied. Readers acknowledge that the author is not engaging in the rendering of legal, financial, medical or professional advice. The content within this book has been derived from various sources. Please consult a licensed professional before attempting any techniques outlined in this book.

By reading this document, the reader agrees that under no circumstances is the author responsible for any losses, direct or indirect, which are incurred as a result of the use of information contained within this document, including, but not limited to, — errors, omissions, or inaccuracies

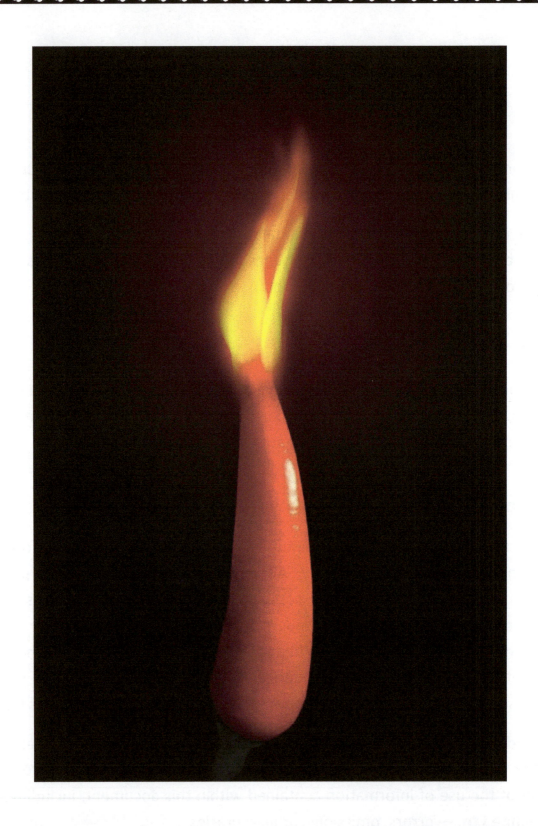

LET'S START!

Table Of Contents

A brief history of chili

140 Delicious Recipes

Simple Turkey Chili	16
Chicken Chili	16
White Turkey Chili	17
Colorado Buffalo Chili	18
Cilantro-Chili Pepper Sauce	18
Justin's Hoosier Daddy Chili	19
Down and Dirty Garlic Chili	20
Vegan Chunky Chili	22
Nicole's Accident Chili	23
Chili Cheese Toast	23
Grandma's Chili	24
Jeff's Chili Con Queso	24
Amazing Hawaiian Chicken Chili	25
Melanie's Chili	26
Chili Bean Soup	26
Pumpkin Turkey Chili	27
Five-Can Chili	27
Fresh Tomato Chili Sauce	28
Spicy Chili French Fries	28
Skyline Chili II	29
Emily's Chipotle Chili	30
Green Chili Stew	30
Flatlander Chili	31
Vegan Chili	31
Chicken and Black Bean Chili	32
Chili Cheese Turnovers	33

Summer Vegetarian Chili 33

Green Chili Chicken Burgers.. 34

Hawaiian-Style Chili 35

Jen's Hearty Three Meat Chili 36

Jammin' Tarheel Chili 37

Cheesy Chili Dip II... 38

Chili Cheese Puff 38

Chicken 'N' Chilies Casserole 39

Zippy Vegetable Chili 39

Mulholland's Idaho Chili 40

Chili with Pulled Beef & Pork for a Crowd 40

Vegan Taco Chili 42

Chili Potato Burritos 42

Turkey-Lentil Chili 43

White Chili II.. 44

White Bean Turkey Chili 44

Spicy Beanless Chili 45

Fried Whole Tilapia with Basil and Chilies 46

Cold Day Chili 47

Green Chili Stew.. 47

Chili Cheddar Biscuits... 48

Lucie's Vegetarian Chili 48

Chili Cheese Dip I.. 49

Green Chili Grilled Cheese 49

White Chili with Chicken 50

Chili-Cumin Bean Salad 50

Pork 'N' Green Chili Tortillas 51

Vegetarian Chili 51

Chili Chicken II 52

Chili Seasoning Mix I 52

Red Zone Chili 53

Zippy Three-Bean Chili 54

Chili III 54

Chili I 55

Chili Cornmeal Crescents 56

Chili-Stuffed Flank Steak 56

Big Game Day Chili 57

Quick and Easy Chicken Chili 58

Fiesta Chili Dogs 58

White Chicken Chili 59

Chili Cheese Dip IV 59

Washabinaros Chili 60

Fiesta Chili Beef and Rice 61

Chunky Pumpkin Chili 62

Holy Trinity Chili 62

Green Chili and Cheese Chicken 63

Meatiest Vegetarian Chili from your Slow Cooker 64

SwansonB® Black Bean, Corn and Turkey Chili 65

Slow Cooker Chicken and Sausage Chili 65

Campbell's® Slow Cooker Hearty Beef and Bean 66

Italian Sausage Chili 67

Quick and Spicy Chili 67

Chili with Ground Pork 68

Tangy Chili 69

Rapid Ragu® Chili 70

Venison Burger and Steak Chili 70

Peanut Butter Chili 71

White Chili I 72

Delilah's Wicked Twelve Alarm Chili 72

Green Chili Casserole 73

Waistline-Friendly Turkey Chili 74

Chicken Skewers with Thai Chili Sauce 75

Tommy's Chili	75
Chili Bean Cheese Omelet	76
Fairuzah's Chili	77
Slow-Cooked Habanero Chili	77
Chili-Topped Taters	78
Hoosier Chili	79
Quick and Easy Chili Dip	79
Chili-Crusted Tri-Tip Roast	80
Black Bean Chili	80
No Tomato Chili	81
Thai Chili Butter Sauce	82
Veggie Vegetarian Chili	82
Killer Chili	83
Terrific Turkey Chili	84
Cheesy Taco Chili	85
Wicked Good Veggie Chili	85
Lentil Chili	86
Chili Verde	86
Chicken Chili II	87
Russian Chili	88
Black Bean Chili	88
Chili Bean Dip	89
Chicken and Two Bean Chili	89
BBQ Chili Pasta	90
Chili Noodle Casserole	91
Green Chili and Corn Dip	91
Camp Chili	92
Chili-ghetti	92
No Beans About It - Chili	93
White Chili I	93
Award Winning Chili	94

Ez's Slow Cooker Hot Chili 94

Slow Cooker Bean Casserole AKA Sweet Chili 95

Easy Chili III 95

Debdoozie's Blue Ribbon Chili 96

Chili II 96

Black Bean Chili 97

Green Chili Stew 97

Texas Style Chili with Spicy Jalapeno Chicken 98

Fruity Chili 98

Bry's Chocolate Lamb Chili 99

Chili Cheese Dip 99

Mean Old Chili.. 100

Grilled Prawns with Garlic-Chili Sauce 100

Peoria Chili 101

Shay's Irish Chili... 101

Texas Chili Beef Slices 102

Touchdown Chili... 103

Slow-Cooked Chili 103

Italian Style Chili.. 104

Jill's Vegetable Chili... 104

Cheesy Chili Dip I 105

A Brief History of Chili

Anyone can create an original pot o' red with the right blueprint, yet that first delicious spoonful only cracks the surface of chili con carne. Dig in and you'll find a culinary rabbit hole of fiery flavors, ingredients, techniques and history. But to fully appreciate where this dish can go, you first need to know where it began.

Soup of the Devil

A shroud of mystery surrounds the beginnings of chili con carne. Southwestern lore dates the origin to the religious trances of the mystic Lady in Blue, Sister María de Ágreda. Sister Maria never left her home country of Spain, yet professed to evangelize savages of the New World by presenting herself before them in hypnotic visions. History cannot explain why in 1629, 50 Jumano Indians walked out of the desert of unsettled West Texas to be baptized. They told stories of an ethereal blue-clad woman who had taught them of God. According to Indian legend, the Lady in Blue also taught them of a fiery red stew, which over the next century came to be known as chili con carne.

Spanish priests took a more hostile view of this peculiarly potent brew, deeming it "soup of the devil" and preaching sermons against indulgence. Suppression only fueled the fire, and by the 19th century chili was a staple among cowboys, ruffians and adventurers on the Western frontier. Bricks of dried beef, fat, spices and peppers were saddlebagged for the trail and reconstituted over the campfire. When these outlaws wound up behind bars, the prisons were serving chili as well.

It happened to be the cheapest slop around. As the Civil War ended, chili's popularity took off. By the turn of the century, Chili Queens lined Market Square in San Antonio, chili powder was widely available and chili joints were popping up across the country. The resulting regional variations led to three distinct styles, and what would become a national chili rivalry.

Texas Red

"It can only truly be Texas Red if it walks the thin line just this side of indigestibility: Damning the mouth that eats it and defying the stomach to digest it, the ingredients are hardly willing to lie in the same pot together."—John Thorne, Simple Cooking. Chili con carne was dubbed the Lone Star's state food in 1977, and they reckon a real bowl o' red hasn't left the state since. Texas Red is a potent, pungent concoction that touts a no-frills approach to chili: just meat, spices and as many chiles as you can stand. To Texans, anything else isn't even called chili.

Springfield-Style "Chilli"

Springfield-style "chilli" is a saucy stew with no fear of a little fat in the mix, often in the form of suet: the hard fat found around the organs of beef or mutton. The Midwesterners go with a mild, cumin-heavy spice mix and usually add a generous helping of beans ("Treason!" says the Texan). It takes no small amount of hubris to rename a dish in your own honor (read: ch-ILLI-nois), but in 1993 the state legislature of Illinois went one step further to name Springfield "The Chilli Capital of the Civilized World." At its peak, Springfield boasted over a dozen chili parlors, three chili canners and exports of over four million cans per year.

Cincinnati Five-Way Chili

In stark contrast to its western cousins, Cincinnati chili is closer to Italian Bolognese than Texas Red. Developed during the Roaring Twenties from Greek roots, this thin chili uses Mediterranean spices such as cinnamon, allspice, cloves and cocoa. Most oddly of all, Cincinnati chili is served over spaghetti with a host of toppings. The traditional Cincinnati Five-Way comes with the works: a loose chili meat sauce, spaghetti noodles, chopped raw onions, red beans and cheese.

What It All Means

Chili began as a no-nonsense dish on the Western frontier, but has evolved into a national pastime. It was no accident that chili established a special place in the belly of America — it has the uncanny ability to turn tough, tired and otherwise tasteless ingredients into a delicious meal through a delightful combination of spices and slow-cooking. To turn nothing into something requires a curious stubbornness that perhaps itself is all too American.

140 DELICIOUS RECIPES

Simple Turkey Chili

Ingredients	Directions
❖ 1 1/2 teaspoons olive oil ❖ 1 pound ground turkey ❖ 1 onion, chopped ❖ 2 cups water ❖ 1 (28 ounce) can canned crushed tomatoes ❖ 1 (16 ounce) can canned kidney beans - drained, rinsed, and ❖ mashed ❖ 1 tablespoon garlic, minced ❖ 2 tablespoons chili powder ❖ 1/2 teaspoon paprika ❖ 1/2 teaspoon dried oregano ❖ 1/2 teaspoon ground cayenne pepper ❖ 1/2 teaspoon ground cumin ❖ 1/2 teaspoon salt ❖ 1/2 teaspoon ground black pepper	Heat the oil in a large pot over medium heat. Place turkey in the pot, and cook until evenly brown. Stir in onion, and cook until tender. Pour water into the pot. Mix in tomatoes, kidney beans, and garlic. Season chili powder, paprika, oregano, cayenne pepper, cumin, salt, and pepper. Bring to a boil. Reduce heat to low, cover, and simmer 30 minutes.

Chicken Chili

Ingredients	Directions
❖ 3 tablespoons vegetable oil ❖ 2 cloves garlic, minced ❖ 1 green bell pepper, chopped ❖ 1 onion, chopped ❖ 1 stalk celery, sliced ❖ 1/4 pound mushrooms, chopped ❖ 1 pound skinless, boneless chicken breast halves - cut into bite size pieces ❖ 1 tablespoon chili powder ❖ 1 teaspoon dried oregano ❖ 1 teaspoon ground cumin ❖ 1/2 teaspoon paprika ❖ 1/2 teaspoon cocoa powder	In a large skillet heat 2 tablespoons of the oil over medium heat. Saute the garlic, bell pepper, onion, celery and mushrooms for 5 minutes. Set aside. Add the remaining 1 tablespoon of oil to the skillet and brown the chicken over high heat until it is golden brown and firm on the outside. Return the vegetable mixture to the skillet. Add the chili powder, cumin, oregano, paprika, cocoa powder, salt, hot pepper flakes and ground black pepper to the

Ingredients	Directions
❖ 1/4 teaspoon salt ❖ 1 pinch crushed red pepper flakes ❖ 1 pinch ground black pepper ❖ 1 (14.5 ounce) can whole peeled tomatoes with juice ❖ 1 (19 ounce) can kidney beans, drained and rinsed	skillet. Stir for a few minutes to prevent burning. Add the tomatoes and beans, bring all to a boil and reduce heat to low. Cover the skillet and simmer for 15 minutes, then remove cover and simmer for 15 more minutes.

White Turkey Chili

Ingredients	Directions
❖ 1 tablespoon olive oil ❖ 1 1/2 cups chopped onion ❖ 3 cloves garlic, minced ❖ 2 teaspoons dried oregano ❖ 1 1/2 teaspoons ground cumin ❖ 1/2 teaspoon ground ginger ❖ 1/2 cup low-sodium chicken broth ❖ 1/2 cup dry white wine ❖ 1 bay leaf ❖ 2 cups shredded cooked turkey ❖ 2 cups white kidney beans (cannellini), undrained ❖ 2 fresh jalapeno peppers, chopped ❖ 1 1/2 cups shredded Monterey Jack cheese ❖ 1/2 teaspoon salt ❖ 1/2 teaspoon coarsely ground black pepper ❖ 2 tablespoons lime juice	Heat the olive oil in a skillet over medium heat. Cook onion in oil until the onion has softened and turned translucent, about 5 minutes. Stir in garlic, oregano, cumin, and ginger; cook for another minute. Pour in chicken broth and white wine, and then add the bay leaf. Cook uncovered until slightly reduced, about 5 to 8 minutes. Stir in turkey, beans, and jalapeno. Simmer uncovered for 10 minutes, stirring occasionally. Using back of spoon, mash 1/4 of beans to thicken sauce. Reduce heat to low, and begin stirring in cheese 1/2 cup at a time. Stir until cheese is completely melted. Season with salt and pepper. Remove from heat, and stir in lime juice. Serve hot.

Colorado Buffalo Chili

Ingredients	Directions
❖ 1 pound ground buffalo ❖ 1 1/2 teaspoons ground cumin ❖ 1/2 teaspoon ground cumin ❖ 1 (10 ounce) can diced tomatoes with green chiles ❖ 1 (10.75 ounce) can tomato soup ❖ 1 (14.5 ounce) can kidney beans, drained ❖ 1 (14.5 ounce) can black beans, drained ❖ 1/2 medium onion, chopped ❖ 1/2 teaspoon minced garlic ❖ 1 Anaheim chile pepper, chopped ❖ 1 poblano chile pepper, chopped ❖ 2 tablespoons chili powder ❖ 1 teaspoon red pepper flakes salt and pepper to taste	Brown the buffalo in a skillet over medium heat; season with 1/2 teaspoon cayenne pepper and 1/2 teaspoon cumin; drain. Combine the buffalo, tomatoes with green chiles, tomato soup, kidney beans, black beans, onion, garlic, Anaheim chile pepper, poblano chile pepper, chili powder, red pepper flakes, black pepper, and salt in a slow cooker. Cover and cook on Low overnight or 8 hours.

Cilantro-Chili Pepper Sauce

Ingredients	Directions
❖ 3 fresh red chile peppers ❖ 1 tablespoon sesame oil ❖ 3 cloves garlic, minced ❖ 1 pinch kosher salt ❖ 1/2 cup malt vinegar ❖ 2 tablespoons fish sauce ❖ 2 tablespoons brown sugar ❖ 3 tablespoons soy sauce ❖ 1 teaspoon lime juice ❖ 1 bunch cilantro, chopped ❖ 1 green onion, chopped	Cut the stem end off of the chile peppers, and remove the seeds using a thin knife, otherwise leaving the peppers whole. Place the peppers into a skillet, and toast over medium-high heat, turning frequently, until the skins of the peppers have blackened and loosened, about 10 minutes. The peppers are ready when 1/4 of the skin has blackened. Remove the peppers, place into a small bowl, and cover with plastic wrap. Allow to cool and steam for about 15 minutes, then remove and discard the skins. Chop the peppers, and set aside. Heat the sesame oil in the skillet

over medium heat. Stir in the garlic, and cook for 2 minutes to soften, then increase heat to medium-high, and stir in the chopped peppers and salt. Cook and stir until the mixture is hot and sizzling, about 1 minute. Pour in the vinegar, brown sugar, and fish sauce. Bring to a boil, then reduce heat to medium-low, and allow to simmer for 10 minutes.

Scrape the mixture into a blender, and add the soy sauce, lime juice, cilantro, and green onion. Puree until smooth. Serve immediately.

Justin's Hoosier Daddy Chili

Ingredients	Directions
❖ 1 pound ground beef ❖ 1 medium onion, chopped ❖ 1 teaspoon red pepper flakes ❖ 1 tablespoon ground cumin ❖ 2 (10.75 ounce) cans condensed tomato soup ❖ 2 (14.5 ounce) cans chicken broth ❖ 1 (14.5 ounce) can crushed tomatoes ❖ 5 tablespoons chili powder ❖ 1 teaspoon ground black pepper ❖ 1 teaspoon salt ❖ 2 (15.5 ounce) cans pinto beans, drained (optional) ❖ cayenne pepper to taste	Crumble the ground beef into a soup pot over medium-high heat. Cook and stir until evenly browned. Drain off most of the grease. Add onion, red pepper flakes, and half of the cumin; cook and stir until onion is tender. Pour in the tomato soup, chicken broth, and crushed tomatoes. Season with chili powder, salt and pepper. Simmer for 30 minutes. Pour in the beans, and season with remaining cumin and cayenne pepper; simmer for another 30 minutes. Now enjoy.

Down and Dirty Garlic Chili

Ingredients	Directions
❖ 1 pound extra lean ground beef ❖ 1 tablespoon chili powder ❖ 2 tablespoons dried onion flakes ❖ 1 teaspoon ground cumin ❖ 1 teaspoon paprika ❖ 2 cloves garlic, minced ❖ 1/4 teaspoon red pepper flakes, or to taste ❖ 1 (14.5 ounce) can diced tomatoes with garlic and onion ❖ 1 (16 ounce) can chili beans, drained ❖ 1 (8 ounce) can tomato sauce salt and pepper to taste	Heat a large saucepan or Dutch oven over medium heat. Add ground beef, and cook until evenly browned. Stir occasionally to crumble. Season the beef with chili powder, onion flakes, cumin, paprika, garlic and red pepper flakes, and mix well. Pour in the tomatoes, chili beans, and tomato sauce. Reduce heat to low, and simmer for at least 30 minutes, or longer for thicker chili. Season to taste with salt and pepper.

Vegan Chunky Chili

Ingredients	Directions
<ul><li>1/2 cup dry kidney beans, soaked overnight</li><li>1/2 cup dry white beans, soaked overnight</li><li>1/2 cup dry brown lentils, soaked overnight</li><li>6 cups chopped fresh tomatoes</li><li>6 cups water</li><li>1 cup chopped fresh mushrooms</li><li>1/2 cup chopped green bell</li><li>pepper</li><li>1/2 cup chopped red bell pepper</li><li>1/2 cup fresh green beans</li><li>1/2 cup chopped celery</li><li>1/4 onion, chopped</li><li>1/4 red onion, chopped</li><li>3/4 cup extra firm tofu, drained, crumbled</li><li>salt to taste</li><li>black pepper to taste onion powder to taste garlic powder to taste chili powder to taste</li></ul>	Drain and rinse kidney beans, white beans and lentils. Combine in a large pot and cover with water; boil over medium-high to high heat for 1 hour, or until tender. Meanwhile, in a large saucepan over high heat, combine tomatoes and water; bring to a boil. Reduce heat to low and simmer, uncovered, for 1 hour, or until tomatoes are broken down. Stir the tomatoes into the beans and add mushrooms, green bell pepper, red bell pepper, green beans, celery, onions and tofu. Season with salt, pepper, onion powder, garlic powder and chili powder to taste. Simmer for 2 to 3 hours, or until desired consistency is reached.

Nicole's Accident Chili

Ingredients	Directions
❖ 1 pound ground beef ❖ 1 teaspoon onion, chopped ❖ 1 (16 ounce) can red kidney beans, drained ❖ 1 (46 fluid ounce) can canned vegetable juice ❖ 1 (8 ounce) can tomato sauce ❖ 1 (6 ounce) can tomato paste ❖ 1 (14.5 ounce) can stewed tomatoes ❖ 2 teaspoons salt garlic powder to taste ground black pepper to taste	In a skillet over medium heat, brown the ground beef and cook the onion until tender. Drain grease. In a pot, mix the beef and onion, beans, vegetable juice, tomato sauce, tomato paste, and tomatoes. Season with salt, garlic powder, and pepper. Bring to a boil, reduce heat to low, cover, and simmer 45 minutes, stirring occasionally.

Chili Cheese Toast

Ingredients	Directions
❖ 1 (4 ounce) can chopped green chilies ❖ 2 tablespoons mayonnaise ❖ 6 slices French bread, toasted ❖ 6 slices Monterey Jack or pepper jack cheese	In a bowl, combine the chilies and mayonnaise. Spread over each slice of bread. Top each with a cheese slice. Broil 4 in. from the heat for 3-4 minutes or until cheese is melted.

Grandma's Chili

Ingredients	Directions
❖ 2 pounds ground beef ❖ 1/2 onion, chopped ❖ 1/2 green bell pepper, chopped salt and pepper to taste ❖ 1 (15 ounce) can baked beans ❖ 1 (4.5 ounce) can mushrooms, drained ❖ 1 tablespoon brown sugar ❖ 1/4 teaspoon chili powder	In a large saucepan over medium high heat, saute the ground beef for 5 minutes, or until browned. Stir in the onion and green bell pepper and saute for 5 more minutes. Season with salt and pepper to taste. Next, add the beans, mushrooms, brown sugar and chili powder to taste. Mix together well, reduce heat to low and let simmer for 20 minutes to 1 hour or more, depending on how much time you have and how thick you like your chili.

Jeff's Chili Con Queso

Ingredients	Directions
❖ 1 (8 ounce) package processed American cheese, cubed ❖ 1 (8 ounce) package mild Cheddar cheese, cubed ❖ 1 (7 ounce) can mild, chunky salsa ❖ 3/4 (15 ounce) can chili ❖ 1 (8 ounce) container sour cream ❖ 1 teaspoon chili powder ❖ 1 dash hot pepper sauce	In a medium saucepan over low heat, melt the processed American cheese and Cheddar cheese. When cheeses are melted and thoroughly blended, mix in salsa, chili, sour cream, chili powder and hot pepper sauce. Cook and stir 10 to 15 minutes before serving warm

Amazing Hawaiian Chicken Chili

Ingredients	Directions
❖ 2 pounds skinless, boneless chicken breast halves ❖ 1 cup barbeque sauce ❖ 2 tablespoons butter, divided ❖ 1 large onion, diced ❖ 2 cloves garlic, minced ❖ 1 large roasted red pepper, chopped ❖ 1 (6 ounce) can tomato paste ❖ 3 tablespoons chili powder ❖ 1 tablespoon ancho chile powder ❖ 1 tablespoon ground cumin ❖ 1 teaspoon ground ginger ❖ 1 tablespoon vanilla extract ❖ 1/2 teaspoon white sugar ❖ 1 (20 ounce) can pineapple chunks ❖ 1 (15 ounce) can kidney beans, drained ❖ 1 (15 ounce) can black beans, drained ❖ 1 (28 ounce) can chopped tomatoes, drained ❖ 1 (24 ounce) jar chipotle salsa salt and pepper to taste	Place the chicken breasts and barbecue sauce in a gallon-sized zip top bag and allow to marinate for 30 minutes in the refrigerator. Melt 1 tablespoon of butter in a large skillet placed over high heat, and add the chicken. Cook the chicken until it is browned and almost cooked through, about 5 minutes per side. Remove chicken from skillet, chop into 1 inch pieces, and place in the crock of a slow cooker. Heat the remaining 1 tablespoon of butter in the skillet over medium-high heat, add the diced onion, garlic, and roasted red pepper, and cook and stir until the onion is softened, about 5 minutes. Stir in the tomato paste, chili powder, ancho chile powder, ground cumin, ground ginger, vanilla, and sugar. Cook, stirring, until blended, about 2 minutes. Transfer the mixture to the slow cooker. Drain the canned pineapple and reserve the fruit. Stir the pineapple juice, kidney beans, black beans, tomatoes, and chipotle salsa into the ingredients in the slow cooker and set the heat to High. Allow the chili to cook on High until it begins to bubble, about 20 minutes. Turn the slow cooker to Low and cook for 1 additional hour. Stir the reserved pineapple into the chili and continue to cook until the pineapple is warm, about 15 minutes. Salt and pepper the chili to taste and serve piping hot.

Melanie's Chili

Ingredients	Directions
❖ 1 pound ground beef ❖ 1 onion, chopped ❖ 1 (14.5 ounce) can diced tomatoes ❖ 1 (15 ounce) can tomato sauce ❖ 1 (16 ounce) can pinto beans ❖ 1 teaspoon chili powder ❖ 1 teaspoon ground cumin ❖ 1/2 teaspoon ground cayenne pepper ❖ 1 teaspoon minced garlic	In a large saucepan over medium-high heat, cook beef and onion until meat is no longer pink. Stir in tomatoes, tomato sauce, beans, chili powder, cumin, cayenne and garlic. Cover, reduce heat and simmer 20 minutes.

Chili Bean Soup

Ingredients	Directions
❖ 1 medium onion, chopped ❖ 3 garlic cloves, minced ❖ 3 tablespoons olive or vegetable oil ❖ 4 cups vegetable broth ❖ 1 (16 ounce) can kidney beans, rinsed and drained ❖ 1 (4 ounce) can chopped green chilies ❖ 1/4 cup tomato paste ❖ 1 tablespoon soy sauce ❖ 1 tablespoon Worcestershire sauce ❖ 1 1/2 teaspoons brown sugar ❖ 1 1/2 teaspoons lime juice ❖ 1 teaspoon dried basil ❖ 1 teaspoon dried oregano ❖ 1 teaspoon ground cumin	In a large saucepan, saute onion and garlic in oil until tender. Stir in remaining ingredients. Bring to a boil. Reduce heat; simmer, uncovered, for 15 minutes or until heated through.

Pumpkin Turkey Chili

Ingredients	Directions
❖ 1 tablespoon vegetable oil ❖ 1 cup chopped onion ❖ 1/2 cup chopped green bell pepper ❖ 1/2 cup chopped yellow bell pepper ❖ 1 clove garlic, minced ❖ 1 pound ground turkey ❖ 1 (14.5 ounce) can diced tomatoes ❖ 2 cups pumpkin puree ❖ 1 1/2 tablespoons chili powder ❖ 1/2 teaspoon ground black ❖ pepper ❖ 1 dash salt ❖ 1/2 cup shredded Cheddar cheese ❖ 1/2 cup sour cream	Heat the oil in a large skillet over medium heat, and saute the onion, green bell pepper, yellow bell pepper, and garlic until tender. Stir in the turkey, and cook until evenly brown. Drain, and mix in tomatoes and pumpkin. Season with chili powder, pepper, and salt. Reduce heat to low, cover, and simmer 20 minutes. Serve topped with Cheddar cheese and sour cream.

Five-Can Chili

Ingredients	Directions
❖ 1 (15 ounce) can chili with beans ❖ 1 (15 ounce) can mixed ❖ vegetables, drained ❖ 1 (11 ounce) can whole kernel corn, drained ❖ 1 (10.75 ounce) can condensed tomato soup, undiluted ❖ 1 (10 ounce) can diced tomatoes and green chilies	In a saucepan, combine all ingredients; heat through.

Fresh Tomato Chili Sauce

Ingredients	Directions
❖ 35 fresh tomatoes, peeled, seeded and chopped ❖ 3 fresh hot chile peppers, seeded and chopped ❖ 4 red bell peppers, cored, seeded and cut into 2-inch pieces ❖ 1 large onion, chopped ❖ 2 cups apple cider vinegar ❖ 1/3 cup fresh lime juice, or amount to taste ❖ 1 cup white sugar ❖ 1 cup packed brown sugar ❖ 1 tablespoon salt, or amount to taste	Place the tomatoes in a large pot over medium heat, and simmer 1 hour. Skim off any excess liquid or foam. Stir in the chile peppers, bell peppers, onion, vinegar, lime juice, white sugar, brown sugar, and desired amount of salt. Reduce heat to low, and simmer 3 to 5 hours until liquid reduces and thickens. Adjust seasonings to taste. Remove chili sauce from heat, and skim off any foam. Pour into hot, sterilized jars, leaving 1/4 inch headroom. Adjust lids. Process for 10 minutes in a boiling-water bath.

Spicy Chili French Fries

Ingredients	Directions
❖ 4 large russet potatoes, peeled and cut into 1/4 inch thick fries ❖ 1/4 cup vegetable oil ❖ 1/4 cup tomato-vegetable juice cocktail ❖ 1 tablespoon chili powder ❖ 1 teaspoon ground cumin ❖ 2 teaspoons dried onion granules ❖ 1 teaspoon garlic powder ❖ 1 teaspoon cayenne pepper ❖ 1 teaspoon white sugar ❖ 1 tablespoon salt	Preheat an oven to 375 degrees F (190 degrees C). Grease a large baking sheet. Fill a large bowl with cold water, add the potatoes, and allow to soak for 10 minutes. Whisk together the oil, vegetable juice cocktail, chili powder, ground cumin, onion granules, garlic powder, cayenne pepper, sugar, and salt in a large bowl. Drain the potatoes, and pat dry with paper towels. Toss the potatoes with the oil and spice mixture; stir until evenly coated. Arrange fries in a single layer on the prepared baking sheet. Bake fries in preheated oven for 20 minutes. Turn and continue to bake until

	browned and crispy, about 20 additional minutes.

Skyline Chili II

Ingredients	Directions
❖ 2 pounds lean ground beef ❖ 2 onions, minced ❖ 35 black peppercorns ❖ 6 bay leaves, crushed ❖ 4 whole dried red chile peppers, seeded and diced ❖ 1/4 teaspoon crushed red pepper flakes ❖ 2 cloves garlic ❖ 1 (6 ounce) can tomato paste ❖ 3 cups water ❖ 4 tablespoons chili powder ❖ 1 teaspoon ground cayenne pepper ❖ 2 1/2 tablespoons distilled white vinegar ❖ 1 1/2 teaspoons ground cinnamon ❖ 1 1/2 teaspoons ground allspice ❖ 1 teaspoon Worcestershire sauce ❖ 1 teaspoon salt ❖ 1 cup shredded Colby cheese	Brown ground beef in skillet with onions. Drain fat. Place the whole peppercorns, bay leaves, small red peppers, and crushed red pepper in a spice bag. In a large pot combine the garlic, tomato paste, water, chili powder, ground red pepper, vinegar, cinnamon, allspice, Worcestershire sauce and salt with the ground beef, onions and spice bag. Cook over low heat for 3 to 4 hours. When ready to serve, don't forget to remove spice bag and whole garlic cloves.

Emily's Chipotle Chili

Ingredients	Directions
❖ 1 pound bulk hot Italian sausage ❖ 2 pounds ground beef ❖ 5 tablespoons chili powder ❖ 1 tablespoon ground cumin ❖ 1 teaspoon ground coriander ❖ 2 cloves garlic, minced ❖ 1 large onion, diced ❖ 1 (28 ounce) can diced tomatoes ❖ 1 (15 ounce) can tomato sauce ❖ 1 (14 ounce) can kidney beans (optional) ❖ 2 teaspoons minced chipotle peppers in adobo sauce ❖ 1 teaspoon salt ❖ ground black pepper ❖ 1 (6 ounce) can tomato paste	Cook sausage and ground beef in a large pot over medium-high heat until lightly browned and crumbly. When the meat has released its grease, and has begun to brown, drain off accumulated grease, and season with chili powder, cumin, and coriander. Cook and stir for 1 minute until fragrant, then stir in the garlic and onion. Cook until the onion has softened and turned translucent, about 4 minutes. Stir in the diced tomatoes, tomato sauce, kidney beans, chipotle peppers, salt, and pepper. Bring to a simmer, and then pour the chili into a slow cooker. Cover, and cook on Low for 8 to 10 hours. Stir in tomato paste an hour before the chili is done.

Green Chili Stew

Ingredients	Directions
❖ 1 tablespoon vegetable oil ❖ 2 pounds cubed beef stew meat ❖ 1 onion, chopped ❖ 1 (10 ounce) can diced tomatoes with green chile peppers ❖ 1 1/2 cups beef broth ❖ 1 (4 ounce) can chopped green chile peppers ❖ 1 teaspoon garlic salt ❖ 1 teaspoon ground cumin salt to taste ❖ ground black pepper to taste ❖ 2 large potatoes, peeled and cubed	In a large pot over medium heat, heat the oil and brown the stew meat and the onions until onions are translucent; about 5 minutes Pour in the diced tomatoes with chiles, beef broth and chile peppers. Stir in the garlic salt and cumin. Salt and pepper to taste. Bring to a boil, reduce heat and simmer for 1 hour. Add a little more beef broth or water if needed during simmering. Stir in cubed potatoes to the mixture and simmer for an additional 30 minutes or until potatoes are tender.

Flatlander Chili

Ingredients	Directions
❖ 2 pounds lean ground beef ❖ 1 (46 fluid ounce) can tomato juice ❖ 1 (29 ounce) can tomato sauce ❖ 1 1/2 cups chopped onion ❖ 1/2 cup chopped celery ❖ 1/4 cup chopped green bell pepper ❖ 1/4 cup chili powder ❖ 2 teaspoons ground cumin ❖ 1 1/2 teaspoons garlic powder ❖ 1 teaspoon salt ❖ 1/2 teaspoon ground black pepper ❖ 1/2 teaspoon dried oregano ❖ 1/2 teaspoon white sugar ❖ 1/8 teaspoon ground cayenne pepper ❖ 2 cups canned red beans, drained and rinsed	Place ground beef in a large, deep skillet. Cook over medium-high heat until evenly brown. Drain, crumble, and set aside. Add all ingredients to a large kettle. Bring to boil. Reduce heat and simmer for 1 to 1 1/2 hours, stirring occasionally.

Vegan Chili

Ingredients	Directions
❖ 1 (12 ounce) package vegetarian burger crumbles ❖ 1 (15 ounce) can tomato sauce ❖ 1 cup water ❖ 1 small onion, chopped ❖ 3 cloves garlic, minced ❖ 1 tablespoon vegetarian Worcestershire sauce ❖ 1 teaspoon liquid smoke flavoring ❖ 2 teaspoons chili powder ❖ 1/8 teaspoon black pepper ❖ 1 teaspoon dry mustard ❖ 1 teaspoon salt ❖ 1/8 teaspoon red pepper flakes	In a large pot combine crumbles, tomato sauce, water, onion, garlic, Worcestershire sauce, liquid smoke, chili powder, black pepper, mustard, salt and pepper flakes. Cook on low heat for 30 minutes, or until heated through.

Chicken and Black Bean Chili

Ingredients	Directions
❖ 2 tablespoons cooking oil ❖ 3 large skinless, boneless chicken breast halves - cut into 1 inch ❖ pieces ❖ sea salt to taste ❖ 1 tablespoon chili powder, or to taste ❖ 1/2 tablespoon ground cumin, or to taste ❖ 1 dried chipotle chili pepper, ground into powder ❖ ground black pepper to taste 1/2 teaspoon ground cayenne pepper ❖ 1 small yellow onion, diced ❖ 1 medium green bell pepper, diced ❖ 1 medium yellow bell pepper, diced ❖ 5 cups water ❖ 1 (15 ounce) can kidney beans, undrained ❖ 1 (15 ounce) can black beans, undrained ❖ 1 (11 ounce) can whole kernel corn, drained ❖ 1 teaspoon green pepper sauce (e.g., TabascoB®) ❖ 1 (6 ounce) can roasted garlic tomato paste ❖ 1 bunch fresh cilantro, chopped	Heat the oil in a large pot over medium heat. Place chicken in the pot; brown on all sides. Season with sea salt, chili powder, cumin, ground chipotle, black pepper, and cayenne pepper. Mix in onion, green bell pepper, and yellow bell pepper. Pour in about 3 cups water, and continue cooking 10 minutes, until about 1/2 the water has evaporated. Mix the kidney beans, black beans, and corn into the pot. Season with green pepper sauce. Reduce heat to low, and mix in remaining 2 cups water and tomato paste. Simmer, stirring occasionally 30 minutes, or until thickened. Top with cilantro to serve

Chili Cheese Turnovers

Ingredients	Directions
❖ 2 (10 ounce) containers refrigerated pizza crust ❖ 2 cups shredded Mexican cheese blend ❖ 1 (15 ounce) can chili without beans ❖ 1 (15 ounce) can ranch-style beans or chili beans, drained ❖ 1 (10 ounce) can diced tomatoes with green chilies, drained ❖ 1 cup sour cream	On a lightly floured surface, press pizza dough into two 12-inch squares. Cut each into four 6-inch squares. In a bowl, combine the cheese, chili and beans. Spoon 1/2 cup in the center of each square. Fold dough diagonally over filling; press edges to seal. Place in two greased 15-in. x 10-in. x 1-in baking pans. Bake at 425 degrees F for 13-18 minutes or until golden brown. Cool for 5 minutes. Meanwhile, in a small bowl, combine tomatoes and sour cream. Serve with turnovers.

Summer Vegetarian Chili

Ingredients	Directions
❖ 2 tablespoons extra-virgin olive oil ❖ 1 cup chopped red onion ❖ 5 large cloves garlic, crushed or minced ❖ 2 tablespoons chili powder, or more to taste ❖ 2 teaspoons ground cumin ❖ 2 cups juicy chopped fresh tomatoes ❖ 1 (15 ounce) can no-salt-added black beans, drained ❖ 1 cup water (or red wine) ❖ 1 cup chopped bell pepper (any color) ❖ 1 cup chopped zucchini ❖ 1 cup corn kernels ❖ 1 cup chopped white or portobello mushrooms ❖ 1 cup chopped fresh cilantro,	Heat oil in medium pot. Add onion, garlic, chili powder and cumin. Saute over medium heat until onion is soft, about 5 minutes. Add remaining ingredients (except garnishes) and stir. Bring to a boil, then lower heat and simmer 20 minutes or until vegetables are soft. Add more liquid if needed. Serve alone or over rice (preferably brown). Garnish if desired with any of the following: reduced-fat cheddar cheese, onion, fat-free sour cream, guacamole, fresh cilantro.

- packed
- ❖ 1/8 teaspoon cayenne pepper, or more to taste
- ❖ Salt and freshly ground black pepper, to taste

Green Chili Chicken Burgers

Ingredients	Directions
❖ 1 avocado, peeled and pitted ❖ 1/2 cup fresh cilantro leaves ❖ 2 tablespoons reduced-fat sour cream ❖ 1/2 teaspoon chili powder salt and pepper to taste ❖ 1 pound ground chicken breast ❖ 1 (4 ounce) can chopped green chile peppers, drained ❖ 1 fresh jalapeno pepper, seeded if desired and finely diced ❖ 3 green onions, finely chopped ❖ 1 tablespoon dried oregano ❖ 1 teaspoon salt ❖ 1 teaspoon garlic powder ground black pepper to taste ❖ 4 slices Cheddar cheese ❖ 4 hamburger buns, split ❖ 1 cup shredded lettuce ❖ 1/3 cup salsa	To make the guacamole, place the avocado, cilantro, sour cream, chili powder, salt, and pepper in a food processor and pulse until smooth.. Mix chicken, canned chiles, jalapeno pepper, green onions, oregano, salt, garlic powder, and pepper in a bowl. Form the mixture into 4 patties. Preheat an outdoor grill for medium heat. Lightly oil the grill grate. Grill each patty 5 minutes per side, until well done. Move the patties to a cooler area of the grill to keep warm, and top each patty with a slice of Cheddar cheese. Lightly grill the buns while the cheese is melting. Spread the bottom of each bun with guacamole, and top with 1/4 cup of shredded lettuce and a grilled chicken burger. Spoon 1 tablespoon of salsa on each burger and top with the other half of the bun to serve.

Hawaiian-Style Chili

Ingredients	Directions
❖ 2 pounds ground beef ❖ 6 onions, chopped ❖ 2 red bell peppers, seeded and chopped ❖ 2 (16 ounce) cans stewed tomatoes, with juice ❖ 2 (15.5 ounce) cans kidney beans, with liquid ❖ 1 (16 ounce) can tomato sauce ❖ 1 (16 ounce) can pineapple chunks, drained ❖ 2 tablespoons chili powder ❖ 2 teaspoons salt	Heat a large Dutch oven until hot over high heat. Add the ground beef, and cook until barely pink, stirring constantly to break into small pieces. Stir in onions and bell pepper, cook until the meat has browned, and the onions have softened and turned translucent, about 5 minutes. Pour meat into a large mesh strainer and press to expel excess fat. Place meat back into Dutch oven along with stewed tomatoes, kidney beans, tomato sauce, and pineapple chunks; season with chili powder and salt. Bring to a boil, then reduce heat to medium-low and simmer uncovered for 10 minutes, or until chili reaches desired consistency.

Jen's Hearty Three Meat Chili

Ingredients	Directions
❖ 1 pound hot or sweet Italian sausage ❖ 1 pound ground beef ❖ 1/2 onion, chopped ❖ 1 1/2 pounds beef stew meat, cut into 1/2 inch pieces ❖ 1 (28 ounce) can diced tomatoes ❖ 1 (12 fluid ounce) bottle dark beer ❖ 2 cups water ❖ 1/4 cup chili powder, or to taste ❖ 1/4 teaspoon red pepper ❖ 1/4 teaspoon white pepper ❖ 1/4 cup white sugar ❖ 1/2 teaspoon ground cinnamon salt and black pepper to taste ❖ 3 tablespoons tomato paste (optional) ❖ 1 (15 ounce) can kidney beans, rinsed and drained (optional)	Cook and stir sausage in a large skillet over medium heat until browned. Drain; place sausage in a pot large enough to hold all ingredients. In same skillet, cook and stir onion with ground beef over medium heat until beef is browned and onions are tender; drain and add to the large pot. In same skillet, cook and stir stew beef over medium heat until browned. Without draining, pour stew beef into the large pot. Pour tomatoes, beer, and water into the pot with meats. Stir in chili powder, red pepper, white pepper, sugar, and cinnamon. Season to taste with salt and black pepper. Simmer until stew beef is very tender, at least 2 hours, stirring occasionally and adding more water as needed. If you prefer a thicker chili, thicken as needed with tomato paste. If using kidney beans, add them 10 minutes before serving, just in time to heat through.

Jammin' Tarheel Chili

Ingredients	Directions
❖ 2 1/2 pounds ground beef ❖ 3 tablespoons olive oil ❖ 3 stalks celery, diced ❖ 2 large onions, diced ❖ 2 cloves garlic, minced ❖ 1 (29 ounce) can tomato sauce ❖ 1 (28 ounce) can crushed tomatoes ❖ 1 (6 ounce) can mushrooms, drained ❖ 1 1/2 cups dark beer ❖ 2 (16 ounce) cans chili beans, drained ❖ 1 (15 ounce) can kidney beans, drained ❖ 1 tablespoon ground cumin ❖ 1/4 cup chili powder ❖ 2 teaspoons ground coriander ❖ 2 teaspoons cayenne pepper ❖ 1 dash Worcestershire sauce	In a large skillet over medium heat, cook beef until brown. Drain. In a large pot over medium heat, cook celery, onions and garlic in olive oil until onion is translucent. Stir in beef, tomato sauce, tomatoes, mushrooms, beer, chili beans, kidney beans, cumin, chili powder, coriander, cayenne and Worcestershire. Simmer over low heat 3 hours, until flavors are well blended.

Cheesy Chili Dip II

Ingredients	Directions
❖ 1 (15 ounce) can chili ❖ 1 (8 ounce) package cream cheese, cubed ❖ 2 (8 ounce) packages shredded mozzarella cheese ❖ garlic powder to taste ground black pepper to taste	Preheat the broiler. In a shallow, medium baking dish, spread the chili and mix in cream cheese. Microwave on high 1 minute, or until cheese is melted and creamy. Stir in 1/2 the mozzarella cheese, garlic powder and pepper. Microwave on high 1 minute, or until melted. Top the mixture with remaining mozzarella cheese. Broil 5 minutes, or until cheese is bubbly and lightly browned.

Chili Cheese Puff

Ingredients	Directions
❖ 5 eggs ❖ 1/4 cup all-purpose flour ❖ 1/2 teaspoon baking powder ❖ 1 cup cottage cheese ❖ 2 cups shredded Monterey Jack cheese ❖ 1/4 cup butter or margarine, melted ❖ 1 (4 ounce) can chopped green chilies, drained	In a large mixing bowl, beat eggs well. Stir in next five ingredients. Add green chilies. Pour into a greased 8-in. square baking pan. Bake at 350 degrees F for 40-45 minutes or until a knife inserted near the center comes out clean. Serve immediately.

Chicken 'N' Chilies Casserole

Ingredients	Directions
❖ 1 cup sour cream ❖ 1 cup light cream ❖ 1 cup chopped onion ❖ 1 (4 ounce) can chopped green chilies ❖ 1 teaspoon salt ❖ 1/2 teaspoon pepper ❖ 1 (2 pound) package frozen loose-pack hash brown potatoes ❖ 2 1/2 cups cubed cooked chicken ❖ 2 1/2 cups shredded Cheddar cheese, divided	In a large bowl, combine sour cream, light cream, onion, chilies, salt and pepper. Stir in potatoes, chicken and 2 cups of the cheese. Pour into a greased 13-in. x 9-in. x 2-in. baking dish. Bake, uncovered, at 350 degrees F for 1 hour and 15 minutes or until golden brown. Sprinkle with remaining cheese before serving.

Zippy Vegetable Chili

Ingredients	Directions
❖ 1 1/2 cups chopped onions ❖ 3/4 cup chopped sweet red pepper ❖ 3/4 cup chopped green pepper ❖ 1 (14.5 ounce) can vegetable broth ❖ 2 (10 ounce) cans diced tomatoes and green chiles ❖ 1/2 cup salsa ❖ 1 tablespoon chili powder ❖ 1 teaspoon ground cumin ❖ 3/4 teaspoon garlic powder ❖ 1 (15 ounce) can pinto beans, rinsed and drained ❖ 1 cup fresh or frozen corn ❖ 1 cup shredded reduced-fat Cheddar cheese	In a large saucepan, bring onions, peppers and broth to a boil. Reduce heat; cover and simmer for 5 minutes. Add tomatoes, salsa and seasonings; return to a boil. Reduce heat; simmer, uncovered, for 12-15 minutes. Add beans and corn; simmer 5 minutes longer or until heated through, stirring occasionally. Garnish each serving with cheese.

Mulholland's Idaho Chili

Ingredients	Directions
❖ 3 cups dried red beans ❖ 9 cups water ❖ 4 ounces jalapeno peppers, thinly sliced ❖ 1 tablespoon garlic powder ❖ 1 tablespoon ground cumin ❖ 1 1/2 teaspoons dried oregano ❖ 2 pounds ground beef ❖ 1 large onion, chopped ❖ 1 teaspoon salt ❖ 4 (14.5 ounce) cans diced tomatoes ❖ 1 (12 ounce) can tomato paste	Sort and rinse beans, then place into a large pot along with the water, jalapeno peppers, garlic powder, cumin, and oregano. Bring to a boil over high heat, then reduce heat to medium-low, cover, and simmer until the beans are tender, 1 1/2 to 2 hours. Heat a large skillet over medium-high heat, and stir in the ground beef and onion. Cook and stir until the beef is crumbly, evenly browned, and no longer pink. Drain and discard any excess grease. Stir the beef into the simmering beans along with the salt, diced tomatoes, and tomato paste. Return to a simmer, and cook for 15 minutes. Remove from the heat, and allow to stand for a few minutes before serving.

Chili with Pulled Beef & Pork for a Crowd

Ingredients	Directions
❖ 2 (2 pound) flat, boneless beef chuck roasts, patted dry ❖ 8 country-style pork ribs, patted dry ❖ 1/2 cup vegetable oil or other flavorless oil ❖ Salt and freshly ground black pepper ❖ 2 tablespoons ground cumin ❖ 1 cup mild chili powder ❖ 4 teaspoons dried oregano ❖ 4 teaspoons ground cumin ❖ 4 large onions, diced ❖ 2 (28 ounce) cans crushed tomatoes	Adjust oven rack to middle position; heat oven to 450 degrees. Set a large, heavy-duty roasting pan over 2 burners on medium heat. Pour 2 Tbs. oil into a medium bowl. Add half the meat; coat. Generously sprinkle with salt, pepper, and 1Tb. cumin. Repeat entire process with rest of meat. Increase heat under roasting pan to medium-high. Add half the meat; cook until a solid brown crust forms on one side, 4 to 5 minutes.

- ❖ 1 (16 ounce) can crushed tomatoes
- ❖ 12 garlic cloves, minced
- ❖ 2 ounces bittersweet chocolate, coarsely chopped
- ❖ 4 (15.5 ounce) cans pinto or kidney beans, rinsed (optional)

Turn over; cook until a crust again forms, 4 to 5 minutes. Transfer meat to a soup pot. Brown remaining meat; add to soup pot. Set roasting pan aside. Add 2 1/2 cups water to the soup pot and cover with heavy-duty foil, pressing down so foil is concave and touches the meat. Seal foil around the top of the pot so it is airtight; place lid on pot. Heat until you hear pan juices bubble. Set pot in oven. Cook, without checking, 90 minutes (meat should be very tender). Carefully remove from oven and let cool. Shred pork and beef into bite-size pieces, discarding pork bones. Measure meat juices, then add enough water to equal 12 cups.

Meanwhile, in a medium skillet over low heat, slow-toast chili powder, oregano and remaining 4 teaspoons cumin, stirring constantly, until spices are fragrant and darker in color; be careful not to burn. Set roasting pan over two burners on medium-high heat; add remaining 1/4 cup oil. Add onions; saute until soft, 7 to 8 minutes. Add spices, tomatoes, meat and juices. Simmer until flavors are unified, 1 to 1 1/2 hours. Add garlic, chocolate and optional beans; simmer 5 minutes. Serve.

Vegan Taco Chili

Ingredients	Directions
❖ 1 tablespoon olive oil ❖ 1 pound sliced fresh mushrooms ❖ 2 cloves garlic, minced ❖ 1 small onion, finely chopped ❖ 2 stalks celery, chopped ❖ 1 (29 ounce) can tomato sauce ❖ 1 (6 ounce) can tomato paste ❖ 3 (15 ounce) cans kidney beans ❖ 1 (11 ounce) can Mexican-style corn	Heat the oil in a large skillet. Sautee the mushrooms, garlic, onion and celery until tender. Transfer them to a stock pot or slow cooker. Stir in the tomato sauce, tomato paste, beans and Mexican-style corn. Cook for at least an hour to blend the flavors

Chili Potato Burritos

Ingredients	Directions
❖ 4 potatoes, peeled and chopped ❖ 1 cup shredded Colby-Monterey Jack cheese ❖ 2 teaspoons chili powder ❖ 1 teaspoon ground cumin ❖ 1 clove garlic, minced salt and pepper to taste ❖ 8 (6 inch) flour tortillas ❖ 1/2 cup red enchilada sauce	Bring a large pot of salted water to a boil. Add potatoes, and cook until tender but still firm, about 15 minutes. Drain, cool and mash. Preheat oven to 350 degrees F (175 degrees C). In a medium mixing bowl, combine mashed potatoes, 3/4 cup cheese, chili powder, cumin, garlic, salt and pepper. Spoon evenly into tortillas, and roll up. Place rolled tortillas side by side in a 8x8 inch baking pan. Spread enchilada sauce evenly over the top, and sprinkle with remaining cheese. Bake in the preheated oven 15 minutes, or until cheese is bubbly

Turkey-Lentil Chili

Ingredients	Directions
❖ 2 cups dry lentils ❖ 2 quarts vegetable broth ❖ 2 tablespoons extra-virgin olive oil ❖ 4 cloves garlic, minced ❖ 1 large onion, chopped ❖ 2 stalks celery, chopped ❖ 1 pound turkey sausage ❖ 2 tomatoes, peeled, seeded, and chopped ❖ 1 teaspoon ground turmeric ❖ 1 teaspoon ground cumin ❖ 1/2 teaspoon dried thyme leaves ❖ 1 pinch crushed red pepper flakes sea salt to taste ❖ 1 (8 ounce) container plain lowfat yogurt ❖ 1/4 cup chopped fresh parsley for garnish	Bring lentils and vegetable broth to a boil in a large pot over high heat. Reduce heat to medium, and simmer for 10 minutes. Meanwhile, heat the olive oil in a large skillet over medium-high heat. Stir in the garlic, onion, celery, and sausage; cook and stir until the sausage is crumbly and no longer pink, about 10 minutes. Stir in tomatoes, turmeric, cumin, thyme, and red pepper flakes; cook 5 minutes more. Stir the sausage mixture into the simmering lentils. Continue simmering until the lentils are tender, 20 to 30 minutes. Season to taste with salt. Garnish each serving with a dollop of yogurt and a sprinkle of chopped parsley to serve.

White Chili II

Ingredients	Directions
❖ 1 1/2 pounds skinless, boneless chicken breast halves - cubed ❖ 1 bunch green onions, thinly sliced ❖ 1 red bell pepper, chopped ❖ 1 yellow bell pepper, chopped ❖ 4 fresh jalapeno peppers, seeded and minced ❖ 1 clove garlic, minced ❖ 1/2 teaspoon ground ginger ❖ 1/2 teaspoon salt ❖ 1/2 teaspoon dried sage ❖ 1/2 teaspoon ground cumin 1/2 teaspoon ground white pepper ❖ 1 tablespoon olive oil ❖ 3 tablespoons butter 1/4 cup all-purpose flour ❖ 2 cups chicken broth ❖ 2 (14 ounce) cans great Northern beans, undrained	In a large skillet, heat olive oil over medium heat. Add chicken, and saute until cooked through. Remove the chicken from the pan. Saute the onion, red bell pepper, yellow bell pepper, jalapeno chile peppers and garlic in the same skillet. Return the chicken, along with the ginger, salt, sage, cumin and white pepper. Mix thoroughly. In a separate small saucepan or skillet, melt butter or margarine over medium heat. Stir in flour to make a roux. Whisk in the chicken broth and mix all together. Stir this mixture into the sauteed chicken and vegetables. Stir in the beans with can liquid, and simmer all over low heat for 15 to 20 minutes or until cooked and heated through.

White Bean Turkey Chili

Ingredients	Directions
❖ 1 1/2 pounds ground lean turkey ❖ 2 medium onions, chopped ❖ 1 1/2 teaspoons dried oregano ❖ 1 1/2 teaspoons ground cumin ❖ 1 (28 ounce) can diced tomatoes, undrained ❖ 3 cups beef broth ❖ 1 (8 ounce) can tomato sauce ❖ 1 tablespoon chili powder ❖ 1 tablespoon baking cocoa ❖ 2 bay leaves ❖ 1 teaspoon salt	In a Dutch oven or kettle, cook the turkey and onions over medium heat until meat is no longer pink; drain. Add oregano and cumin; cook and stir 1 minute longer. Stir in tomatoes, broth, tomato sauce, chili powder, cocoa, bay leaves, salt and cinnamon. Bring to a boil. Reduce heat; cover and simmer for 45 minutes. Add beans; heat through. Discard bay leaves before serving.

❖ 1/4 teaspoon ground cinnamon ❖ 3 (15 ounce) cans white kidney or cannellini beans, rinsed and ❖ drained	

Spicy Beanless Chili

Ingredients	Directions
❖ 1/2 pound ground beef ❖ 1/3 cup chopped green pepper ❖ 2 tablespoons chopped onion ❖ 1 garlic clove, minced ❖ 1 (8 ounce) can tomato sauce ❖ 1 (5.5 ounce) can tomato juice ❖ 1/2 cup water ❖ 2 tablespoons chili powder ❖ 1/2 teaspoon dried oregano ❖ 1/2 teaspoon paprika ❖ 1/4 teaspoon ground cumin ❖ 1/4 teaspoon cayenne pepper ❖ 1/8 teaspoon salt	In a large saucepan, cook beef, green pepper, onion and garlic over medium heat until meat is no longer pink; drain. Stir in the tomato sauce, tomato juice, water, chili powder, oregano, paprika, cumin and cayenne and salt if desired. Bring to a boil. Reduce heat; simmer, uncovered, for 45 minutes or to desired thickness.

Fried Whole Tilapia with Basil and Chilies

Ingredients	Directions
❖ 1 whole (10 ounce) fresh tilapia, cleaned and scaled ❖ 1 quart oil for deep frying ❖ 2 tablespoons cooking oil ❖ 5 large red chili peppers, sliced ❖ 5 cloves garlic, chopped ❖ 1 yellow onion, chopped ❖ 2 tablespoons fish sauce ❖ 2 tablespoons light soy sauce ❖ 1/4 cup Thai basil leaves ❖ 1/4 cup chopped cilantro	Heat 1 quart oil in a deep-fryer or large saucepan to 350 degrees F (175 degrees C). If you do not have a thermometer, then dip the head of the fish into the oil; if it sizzles, it is ready, if it does not sizzle, then wait a couple minutes and try again. Rinse the fish and dry well. Make several angled slits along the body of the fish, cutting down to the rib bones. Make two lateral slits along the back of the fish, from head to tail, on either side of the dorsal fin. These cuts will ensure quick cooking and maximum crispiness. Gently slip the fish into the oil and fry until crispy, 7 to 10 minutes. Carefully remove the fish from the oil and let it drain on paper towels. Place on a large serving platter. While the fish drains, heat 2 tablespoons oil in a large skillet. Cook and stir the chili peppers, garlic, and onion in the hot oil until lightly browned, 5 to 7 minutes. Stir the fish sauce and soy sauce into the mixture, remove from heat, and fold the Thai basil and cilantro into the mixture. Pour the sauce over the fish to serve.

Cold Day Chili

Ingredients	Directions
❖ 1 pound ground beef ❖ 1 medium onion, halved and thinly sliced ❖ 2 (16 ounce) cans kidney beans, rinsed and drained ❖ 1 (14.5 ounce) can diced tomatoes, undrained ❖ 1/2 cup water ❖ 1 tablespoon brown sugar ❖ 1 tablespoon chili powder ❖ 1 tablespoon vinegar ❖ 2 teaspoons prepared mustard ❖ 1 teaspoon salt ❖ 1/8 teaspoon pepper	In a large saucepan over medium heat, cook beef and onion until the meat is no longer pink; drain. Add the remaining ingredients. Bring to a boil; reduce heat. Cover and simmer for 10 minutes or until heated through.

Green Chili Stew

Ingredients	Directions
❖ 1 1/2 pounds pork neck bones ❖ 2 (7 ounce) cans diced green chiles ❖ 2 pounds potatoes, cubed ❖ 28 ounces chopped stewed tomatoes ❖ 1 large sweet onion, cubed ❖ 3 stalks celery, chopped ❖ 1 teaspoon ground cumin ❖ 2 tablespoons chili powder ❖ 4 cups water	Preheat oven to 400 degrees F (200 degrees C). Place bones into a heavy roasting pan and add enough water to cover bottom of pan. Cover pan with a tight fitting lid and cook until browned. You may need to add more water while it is cooking so be sure to check. In a large stock pot, combine browned boned, chilies, potatoes, tomatoes, onion, celery, cumin, chili pepper and liquid. Simmer for 5 to 6 hours. Remove bones from soup, remove any meat, and place meat back into soup. Once vegetables are tender, serve.

Chili Cheddar Biscuits

Ingredients	Directions
❖ 1 1/3 cups all-purpose flour ❖ 3 teaspoons baking powder ❖ 3 teaspoons dried parsley flakes ❖ 1 teaspoon chili powder ❖ 1/4 teaspoon salt ❖ 1/2 cup cold butter or margarine ❖ 1/2 cup milk ❖ 1 egg, beaten ❖ 1 1/2 cups shredded Cheddar cheese	In a large bowl, combine the dry ingredients. Cut in butter until mixture resembles coarse crumbs. Stir in milk and egg just until moistened. Add cheese; mix well. Turn onto a lightly floured surface. Roll to 1/2-in thickness; cut with a 2-1/2-in. biscuit cutter. Place 1 in. apart on an ungreased baking sheet. Bake at 450 degrees F for 8-10 minutes or until golden brown. Serve warm.

Lucie's Vegetarian Chili

Ingredients	Directions
❖ 1/3 cup olive oil ❖ 2 cups chopped onion ❖ 3/4 cup chopped celery ❖ 1 cup chopped green bell pepper ❖ 1 cup chopped carrots ❖ 1 tablespoon minced garlic ❖ 2 cups chopped mushrooms ❖ 1/4 teaspoon crushed red pepper flakes ❖ 1 tablespoon ground cumin ❖ 2 tablespoons chili powder ❖ 3/4 teaspoon dried basil ❖ 2 teaspoons salt ❖ 1/2 teaspoon ground black pepper ❖ 2 cups tomato juice ❖ 3/4 cup bulgur wheat ❖ 2 cups chopped tomatoes ❖ 1 (20 ounce) can kidney beans, undrained ❖ 1/2 teaspoon hot pepper sauce (such as Tabasco®)	Heat the olive oil in a large pot over high heat. Stir in the onion, celery, green bell pepper, carrot, garlic, mushrooms, red pepper flakes, cumin, chili powder, basil, salt, and pepper. Cook and stir until the vegetables begin to soften, about 2 minutes. Stir in the tomato juice, bulgur wheat, chopped tomatoes, kidney beans, hot pepper sauce, lemon juice, tomato paste, Worcestershire sauce, red wine, and green chile peppers. Bring to a boil, stirring frequently. Reduce heat to medium-low, and simmer, uncovered, 20 minutes before serving.

Ingredients	Directions
❖ 2 tablespoons lemon juice ❖ 3 tablespoons tomato paste ❖ 1 tablespoon Worcestershire sauce ❖ 1/4 cup dry red wine ❖ 2 tablespoons canned chopped green chile peppers, or to taste	

Chili Cheese Dip I

Ingredients	Directions
❖ 60 ounces chili with beans ❖ 2 (8 ounce) packages cream cheese, softened ❖ 2 cups shredded Cheddar cheese	In a slow cooker, combine chili, cream cheese, and Cheddar cheese. Set the slow cooker to a low temperature, and let the dip cook until all of the cheeses have melted. Serve warm.

Green Chili Grilled Cheese

Ingredients	Directions
❖ 4 slices bread ❖ 4 slices Cheddar cheese ❖ 1 (4 ounce) can chopped green chilies, drained ❖ 2 tablespoons butter or margarine, softened	Top two slices of bread with two slices of cheese; sprinkle with chilies. Top with remaining bread. Butter the outsides of sandwiches. In a large skillet over medium heat, cook sandwiches on both sides until golden brown and cheese is melted.

White Chili with Chicken

Ingredients	Directions
❖ 1 medium onion, chopped ❖ 1 jalapeno pepper, seeded and chopped* (optional) ❖ 2 garlic cloves, minced ❖ 1 tablespoon vegetable oil ❖ 4 cups chicken broth ❖ 2 (15.5 ounce) cans great northern beans, rinsed and drained ❖ 2 tablespoons minced fresh parsley ❖ 1 tablespoon lime juice ❖ 1 teaspoon ground cumin ❖ 2 tablespoons cornstarch ❖ 1/4 cup cold water ❖ 2 cups cubed, cooked chicken	In a large saucepan, cook onion, jalapeno if desired and garlic in oil until tender. Stir in broth, beans, parsley, lime juice and cumin; bring to a boil. Reduce heat; cover and simmer for 10 minutes, stirring occasionally. Combine cornstarch and water until smooth; stir into chili. Add chicken. Bring to a boil; cook and stir for 2 minutes or until thickened.

Chili-Cumin Bean Salad

Ingredients	Directions
❖ 4 cups chopped tomatoes ❖ 1 (15 ounce) can yellow hominy, drained ❖ 1 (15 ounce) can black beans, rinsed and drained ❖ 1 (15 ounce) can pinto beans, rinsed and drained ❖ 1 1/2 cups chopped red onion ❖ 1 cup minced fresh cilantro or parsley ❖ 1/4 cup lime juice ❖ 3 tablespoons olive or canola oil ❖ 2 1/2 teaspoons chili powder ❖ 2 1/2 teaspoons ground cumin ❖ 1 teaspoon pepper ❖ 1/2 teaspoon salt	In a large bowl, combine the tomatoes, hominy, beans, onion and cilantro. In a jar with a tight-fitting lid, combine the remaining ingredients; shake well. Pour over salad and toss to coat. Refrigerate for at least 2 hours before serving.

Pork 'N' Green Chili Tortillas

Ingredients	Directions
❖ 1/3 cup all-purpose flour ❖ 1 teaspoon salt ❖ 1/2 teaspoon pepper ❖ 2 pounds pork tenderloin, cubed ❖ 1/4 cup vegetable oil ❖ 6 (4 ounce) cans chopped green chilies ❖ 1/2 cup salsa ❖ 12 (8 inch) flour tortillas Shredded Cheddar cheese	In a large resealable plastic bag, combine the flour, salt and pepper. Add pork cubes and shake to coat. In a large saucepan or skillet, cook pork in oil over medium heat until no longer pink. Add the chilies and salsa. Bring to a boil. Reduce heat; cover and simmer for 30 minutes or until meat is tender. Spoon 1/2 cup onto each tortilla; sprinkle with cheese and roll up.

Vegetarian Chili

Ingredients	Directions
❖ 1 (12 ounce) package frozen burger-style crumbles ❖ 2 (15 ounce) cans black beans, rinsed and drained ❖ 2 (15 ounce) cans dark red kidney beans ❖ 1 (15 ounce) can light red kidney beans ❖ 1 (29 ounce) can diced tomatoes ❖ 1 (12 fluid ounce) can tomato juice ❖ 5 onions, chopped ❖ 3 tablespoons chili powder ❖ 1 1/2 tablespoons ground cumin ❖ 1 tablespoon garlic powder ❖ 2 bay leaves ❖ salt and pepper to taste	In a large pot, combine meat substitute, black beans, kidney beans, diced tomatoes, tomato juice, onions, chili powder, cumin, garlic powder, bay leaves, salt and pepper. Bring to a simmer and cover. Let the chili simmer for at least 1 hour before serving.

Chili Chicken II

Ingredients	Directions
❖ 1/2 teaspoon cider vinegar ❖ 1 teaspoon soy sauce ❖ 2 tablespoons ginger garlic paste ❖ 1 tablespoon chili sauce ❖ salt to taste ❖ 1 pound skinless, boneless chicken breast meat - cut into bite-size pieces ❖ 1 tablespoon vegetable oil ❖ 1 onion, chopped ❖ 1 green bell pepper, chopped ❖ 1 tomato, chopped ❖ 1 teaspoon cornstarch ❖ 1/2 cup water	In a glass dish mix together the vinegar, soy sauce, ginger garlic paste, chili sauce and salt. Place chicken in dish, cover and marinate in the refrigerator for 3 to 4 hours. Remove chicken pieces from dish and set marinade aside. Saute chicken pieces in a small skillet in a little bit of oil. Then heat oil in a medium skillet and saute onions, bell pepper and tomato. Add the marinade and sauteed chicken pieces. Cover skillet and let all simmer for 5 to 7 minutes, or until chicken is cooked through and no longer pink inside. Combine cornstarch and water and mix together to make a paste. Add paste to skillet and stir until mixture thickens.

Chili Seasoning Mix I

Ingredients	Directions
❖ 1 tablespoon paprika ❖ 2 1/2 teaspoons seasoning salt ❖ 1 teaspoon onion powder ❖ 1 teaspoon garlic powder ❖ 1 teaspoon ground cayenne pepper ❖ 1 teaspoon seasoned pepper ❖ 1/2 teaspoon dried thyme ❖ 1/2 teaspoon dried oregano	In a bowl, stir together paprika, seasoning salt, onion powder, garlic powder, cayenne, seasoned pepper, thyme and oregano. Store in an airtight container.

Red Zone Chili

Ingredients	Directions
❖ 1 (12 ounce) package Hebrew NationalB® Beef Franks, sliced ❖ 1/2 pound ground sirloin beef, uncooked ❖ 1 (28 ounce) can Hunt'sB® Petite Diced Tomatoes, undrained ❖ 1 (15 ounce) can Ranch StyleB® Black Beans ❖ 1 (15 ounce) can Ranch StyleB® Pinto Beans ❖ 1 (8 ounce) can Hunt'sB® Tomato Sauce-No Salt Added ❖ 1 cup finely chopped onion ❖ 1 cup finely chopped poblano chile with seeds ❖ 2 tablespoons finely chopped jalapeno chile with seeds ❖ 2 tablespoons GebhardtB® Chili Powder ❖ 1 tablespoon ancho chile powder ❖ 1 tablespoon brown sugar ❖ 1 tablespoon minced garlic ❖ 2 teaspoons ground cumin	Place all ingredients in 4-quart slow cooker; stir to combine thoroughly. Cook on LOW setting 6-1/2 hours or until vegetables are tender.

Zippy Three-Bean Chili

Ingredients	Directions
❖ 1 pound lean ground beef ❖ 1/2 cup chopped onion ❖ 1 cup chopped fresh mushrooms ❖ 1/2 cup chopped green pepper ❖ 1/2 cup chopped sweet red ❖ pepper ❖ 1 clove garlic, minced ❖ 2 cups water ❖ 1 (14.5 ounce) can diced tomatoes and green chilies, undrained ❖ 1 (1.25 ounce) package reduced sodium taco seasoning ❖ 1 (15.5 ounce) can great northern beans, rinsed and drained ❖ 1 (15 ounce) can black beans, rinsed and drained ❖ 1 (15 ounce) can pinto beans, rinsed and drained ❖ 8 tablespoons shredded reduced-fat Cheddar cheese, divided	In a large saucepan, cook beef and onion over medium heat until meat is no longer pink; drain. Add the mushrooms, peppers and garlic; cook and stir 3 minutes longer or until vegetables are almost tender. Stir in the water, tomatoes and taco seasoning. Bring to boil. Reduce heat; simmer, uncovered, for 30 minutes. Add beans; simmer 30 minutes longer. Sprinkle each serving with 1 tablespoon cheese.

Chili III

Ingredients	Directions
❖ 1 pound ground beef ❖ 1 onion, chopped ❖ 2 cups tomato puree ❖ 1 (15 ounce) can kidney beans ❖ 4 potatoes, cubed ❖ 2 1/2 tablespoons chili powder ❖ 2 teaspoons salt ❖ 2 cups water	In a large saucepan over medium high heat, saute the ground beef and the onions about 5 minutes, or until the onions are almost tender. Drain the fat. Add the pureed tomatoes, kidney beans, potatoes, chili powder, salt and water. Reduce heat to low and simmer about 30 minutes, or until potatoes are tender. Add another cup of water if a thinner chili is desired.

Chili I

Ingredients	Directions
❖ 2 tablespoons vegetable oil ❖ 2 onions, chopped ❖ 3 cloves garlic, minced ❖ 1 pound ground beef ❖ 3/4 pound beef sirloin, cubed ❖ 1 (14.5 ounce) can peeled and diced tomatoes with juice ❖ 1 (12 fluid ounce) can or bottle dark beer ❖ 1 cup strong brewed coffee ❖ 2 (6 ounce) cans tomato paste ❖ 1 (14 ounce) can beef broth ❖ 1/2 cup packed brown sugar ❖ 3 1/2 tablespoons chili powder ❖ 1 tablespoon cumin seeds ❖ 1 tablespoon unsweetened cocoa powder ❖ 1 teaspoon dried oregano ❖ 1 teaspoon ground cayenne pepper ❖ 1 teaspoon ground coriander ❖ 1 teaspoon salt ❖ 4 (15 ounce) cans kidney beans ❖ 4 fresh hot chile peppers, seeded and chopped	Heat oil in a large saucepan over medium heat. Cook onions, garlic, ground beef and cubed sirloin in oil for 10 minutes, or until the meat is well browned and the onions are tender. Mix in the diced tomatoes with juice, dark beer, coffee, tomato paste and beef broth. Season with brown sugar, chili powder, cumin, cocoa powder, oregano, cayenne pepper, coriander and salt. Stir in 2 cans of the beans and hot chile peppers. Reduce heat to low, and simmer for 1 1/2 hours. Stir in the 2 remaining cans of beans, and simmer for another 30 minutes.

Chili Cornmeal Crescents

Ingredients	Directions
❖ 1 (.25 ounce) package active dry yeast ❖ 1 3/4 cups warm water (110 degrees to 115 degrees F) 1 egg ❖ 2 tablespoons olive or vegetable oil ❖ 1 1/2 cups cornmeal ❖ 1/3 cup sugar ❖ 1 tablespoon chili powder ❖ 1 teaspoon salt ❖ 4 cups all-purpose flour	In a small bowl, dissolve yeast in water. In a mixing bowl, beat egg and oil. Add cornmeal, sugar, chili powder, salt, yeast mixture and 2 cups flour; mix well. Add enough remaining flour to form a soft dough. Turn onto a floured surface; knead until smooth and elastic, about 6-8 minutes. Place in a greased bowl; turn once to grease top. Cover and let rise in a warm place until doubled, about 1 hour. Punch dough down; divide in half. Roll each portion into a 12-in. circle. Cut into 12 wedges. Roll up each wedge, starting with wide end. Place on greased baking sheet; curve into a crescent shape. Cover and let rise until doubled, about 30 minutes. Bake at 375 degrees F for about 20 minutes or until browned. Cool on wire racks.

Chili-Stuffed Flank Steak

Ingredients	Directions
❖ 1 1/4 pounds lean flank steak, pocket cut ❖ 1 (14.5 ounce) can chili with beans, drained ❖ 1/4 cup canned diced green chiles ❖ 2 teaspoons chili powder ❖ 1 cup low sodium barbecue sauce	Heat a grill to high heat. Place the flank steak on a sheet of heavy duty foil and fill the pocket of the flank steak with chili and diced chilies. Secure the opening of the flank steak with a skewer. Rub the surface of the steak with a thin film of oil (about 2 teaspoons) and season with the chili powder. Clean the grill grate with a metal brush and rub with oil. Put the steak on the grill, cover, and grill to medium-rare, about 8 minutes, turning once halfway through. Coat the flank steak with barbecue sauce and grill another minute on each side.

	Remove skewer, and cut flank steak in thin slices against the grain and serve.

Big Game Day Chili

Ingredients	Directions
❖ 2 tablespoons vegetable oil ❖ 2 yellow onions, chopped ❖ 1 sweet onion, chopped ❖ 1 head garlic, peeled and minced ❖ 1 yellow bell pepper, chopped ❖ 1 orange bell pepper, chopped ❖ 2 pounds cubed beef stew meat ❖ 2 pounds Italian sausage meat ❖ 4 slices applewood smoked bacon, cut into 1-inch pieces ❖ 2 (28 ounce) cans tomato sauce ❖ 2 (6 ounce) cans tomato paste ❖ 2 (14 ounce) cans black beans, rinsed and drained ❖ 2 (14.5 ounce) cans kidney beans, rinsed and drained ❖ 1 (7 ounce) can chipotle peppers in adobo sauce, chopped ❖ 2 cups beef broth ❖ 1 (12 fluid ounce) bottle dark beer ❖ 1/4 teaspoon chili powder, or to taste ❖ 1/4 cup crumbled dried oregano ❖ 1 tablespoon fresh-ground black pepper ❖ 2 teaspoons salt, or amount to taste ❖ 2 1/2 ounces dark chocolate candy bar	Heat the oil in a large deep pot over medium-high heat, and stir in the onions, garlic, and bell peppers. Cook and stir until the onions are transparent, about 5 minutes. Add the beef stew meat, sausage, and bacon. Cook until meats are evenly browned. Drain the fat. Stir in the tomato sauce, tomato paste, black beans, kidney beans, chipotle peppers with sauce, beef broth, beer, chili powder, oregano, pepper, salt, and chocolate. Bring the mixture to a boil. Reduce heat to low and simmer for at least 1 hour; 2 hours is preferred.

Quick and Easy Chicken Chili

Ingredients	Directions
❖ 1 (15.5 ounce) can corn ❖ 1 (15.5 ounce) can white hominy ❖ 2 (15.5 ounce) cans pinto beans ❖ 2 (15.5 ounce) cans kidney beans ❖ 1 (12 ounce) jar salsa ❖ 2 tablespoons chili powder ❖ 2 tablespoons ground cumin ❖ 1 cup water ❖ 1 pound shredded cooked chicken	Stir together the corn, hominy, pinto beans, and kidney beans in a large saucepan over medium heat; bring to a boil. Stir in the salsa, chili powder, cumin, and water; return to a boil. Cook another 15 minutes. Stir in the chicken to serve.

Fiesta Chili Dogs

Ingredients	Directions
❖ 3 (15 ounce) cans chili without beans ❖ 2 (10.75 ounce) cans condensed cheddar cheese soup, undiluted 1/2 cup minced fresh cilantro or parsley, divided ❖ 1 jalapeno pepper, seeded and minced ❖ 2 garlic cloves, minced ❖ 24 hot dogs ❖ 24 hot dog buns, split and toasted ❖ 2 (4 ounce) cans sliced black olives, drained ❖ 1 medium onion, chopped ❖ 3 cups crushed corn chips	In a large saucepan, combine the chili and soup; stir in 1/4 cup cilantro, jalapeno and garlic. Add hot dogs. Bring to a boil. Reduce heat; cover and simmer for 35-40 minutes, stirring occasionally. Stir in the remaining cilantro. To assemble, place hot dogs in buns; top with chili sauce, olives, onion and chips.

White Chicken Chili

Ingredients	Directions
❖ 1 tablespoon vegetable oil ❖ 1 pound skinless, boneless chicken breast, cut into cubes ❖ 1 tablespoon chili powder ❖ 1 (10.75 ounce) can Campbell's® Condensed Cream of Chicken ❖ Soup (Regular or 98% Fat Free) ❖ 2 cups water ❖ 1 pouch Campbell's® Dry Onion Soup and Recipe Mix ❖ 2 (15 ounce) cans white kidney beans (cannellini), rinsed and drained ❖ Shredded Cheddar cheese Sliced green onion	Heat oil in saucepan. Add chicken and chili powder and cook until browned, stirring often. Add chicken soup, water and soup mix. Heat to a boil. Cover and cook over low heat 10 minutes. Add beans and heat through. Garnish with cheese and onions.

Chili Cheese Dip IV

Ingredients	Directions
❖ 1 (15 ounce) can chili without beans ❖ 1 cup shredded Cheddar cheese ❖ 1 (8 ounce) jar chunky salsa ❖ 1 (2.25 ounce) can chopped black olives, drained ❖ 1 (18 ounce) package tortilla chips	In a medium microwave safe bowl, mix chili without beans, Cheddar cheese, chunky salsa, and black olives. Microwave the mixture on High approximately 3 minutes, until cheese begins to melt. Stir the mixture, and return to microwave. Continue cooking in microwave in 1 to 3 minute intervals, until thoroughly blended and hot. Serve with tortilla chips.

Washabinaros Chili

Ingredients	Directions
❖ 4 tablespoons vegetable oil, divided ❖ 2 onions, chopped ❖ 4 cloves garlic, minced ❖ 1 pound ground beef ❖ 3/4 pound spicy Italian sausage, casing removed ❖ 1 (14.5 ounce) can peeled and diced tomatoes with juice ❖ 1 (12 fluid ounce) can or bottle dark beer ❖ 1 cup strong brewed coffee ❖ 2 (6 ounce) cans tomato paste ❖ 1 (14 ounce) can beef broth ❖ 1/4 cup chili powder ❖ 1 tablespoon ground cumin ❖ 1/4 cup brown sugar ❖ 1 teaspoon dried oregano ❖ 1 teaspoon cayenne pepper ❖ 1 teaspoon ground coriander ❖ 1 teaspoon salt ❖ 1 tablespoon wasabi paste ❖ 3 (15 ounce) cans kidney beans ❖ 2 Anaheim chile peppers, chopped ❖ 1 serrano pepper, chopped ❖ 1 habanero pepper, sliced	Place 2 tablespoons of oil in a large pot and place the pot over medium heat. Cook and stir the onions, garlic, beef and sausage until meats are browned. Pour in the tomatoes, beer, coffee, tomato paste and broth. Season with chili powder, cumin, sugar, oregano, cayenne, coriander, salt and wasabi. Stir in one can of beans, bring to a boil, then reduce heat, cover and simmer. In a large skillet over medium heat, heat remaining oil. Cook Anaheim, serrano and habanero peppers in oil until just tender, 5 to 10 minutes. Stir into the pot and simmer 2 hours. Stir in remaining 2 cans of beans and cook 45 minutes more.

Fiesta Chili Beef and Rice

Ingredients	Directions
❖ 2 tablespoons vegetable oil ❖ 1 cup white rice ❖ 1 cup chopped onion ❖ 1 cup chopped green bell pepper ❖ 1 1/4 cups water ❖ 1 (10 ounce) can red chile sauce ❖ 1 (8.75 ounce) can sweet corn ❖ 1 tablespoon lemon juice ❖ 1 teaspoon salt ❖ 1 pound sirloin, cut into 1 inch cubes ❖ 1 (15 ounce) can Mexican-style tomato sauce ❖ 1 teaspoon ground cumin ❖ 1 cup shredded Monterey Jack cheese	Add oil to a medium saucepan. Stir in rice, and cook over medium heat until rice begins to have a golden color, about 5 minutes. Add 1/2 cup onion and 1/2 cup green pepper; cook and stir for 1 minute. Stir in water and half of the chili sauce. Bring to boil. Mix in corn, lemon juice, and 1/2 teaspoon salt. Cover, and simmer over low heat for 20 minutes. Meanwhile, saute beef with remaining 1/2 cup onion and 1/2 cup green pepper until meat loses pink color and vegetables are tender. Add remaining chili sauce, tomato sauce, cumin, and 1/2 teaspoon salt. Simmer uncovered 15 minutes. Turn rice onto a platter, and fluff with a fork. Sprinkle with cheese, and top with beef mixture. Serve immediately.

Chunky Pumpkin Chili

Ingredients	Directions
❖ 2 pounds ground beef ❖ 1 large onion, diced ❖ 1 green bell pepper, diced ❖ 2 (15 ounce) cans kidney beans, drained ❖ 1 (46 fluid ounce) can tomato juice ❖ 1 (28 ounce) can peeled and diced tomatoes with juice ❖ 1/2 cup canned pumpkin puree ❖ 1 tablespoon pumpkin pie spice ❖ 1 tablespoon chili powder ❖ 1/4 tablespoon SPLENDA® No Calorie Sweetener, Granulated	In a large pot over medium heat, cook beef until brown; drain. Stir in onion and bell pepper and cook 5 minutes. Stir in beans, tomato juice, diced tomatoes and pumpkin puree. Season with pumpkin pie spice, chili powder and SPLENDA® Granulated Sweetener. Simmer 1 hour.

Holy Trinity Chili

Ingredients	Directions
❖ 2 pounds ground beef ❖ 1 (12 ounce) package smoked sausages, cut into bite-sized pieces ❖ 9 slices bacon, diced ❖ 2 tablespoons minced garlic ❖ 2 onions, diced ❖ 1 (6 ounce) can tomato paste ❖ 1 (14 ounce) can beef broth ❖ 1 (28 ounce) can diced tomatoes ❖ 1 (15 ounce) can mild chili beans, with sauce ❖ 2 (15 ounce) cans pinto beans, drained ❖ 3 Anaheim (New Mexico) chile peppers, seeded and minced ❖ 3 jalapeno peppers, seeded and minced ❖ 3 serrano peppers, seeded and minced	Brown the ground beef in a large soup pot over medium-high heat until cooked and crumbly; drain and set aside. Brown sausages, and then set aside. Reduce heat to medium and stir in bacon. Cook until the bacon has released its fat and is beginning to turn crispy. Stir in garlic and onions, and cook until the onions soften and turn translucent, about 5 minutes. Stir in tomato paste to coat the onions. Pour in beef broth, diced tomatoes, chili beans, and pinto beans. Add the Anaheim peppers, jalapeno peppers, and serrano peppers. Season with Worcestershire, brown sugar, chipotle powder, and cumin. Bring to a boil over high heat, then reduce heat to medium-low, and simmer for 2 hours, or until thickened, stirring occasionally. Season to taste with salt and pepper, then simmer for 5 additional

❖ 3 tablespoons Worcestershire sauce ❖ 1/3 cup brown sugar ❖ 2 teaspoons chipotle chile powder ❖ 2 teaspoons ground cumin salt and pepper to taste	minutes before serving.

Green Chili and Cheese Chicken

Ingredients	Directions
❖ 4 boneless, skinless chicken breasts ❖ 1 1/2 cups shredded pepperjack cheese ❖ 1 (4 ounce) can diced green chile peppers, drained ❖ 1 tablespoon dry fajita seasoning	Preheat the oven to 350 degrees F (175 degrees C). Coat a 9 inch square baking dish (or similar size) with cooking spray. Make a deep cut into the side of each chicken breast half to form a pocket or 'purse'. Stuff 1/4 cup of cheese and about 1 tablespoon of the chilies onto each one. Close, and secure with a toothpick so that the cheese does not escape while in the oven. Place the stuffed chicken into the baking dish. Season with Fajita seasoning, and then sprinkle the remaining cheese and chilies over the top. Bake uncovered for 30 minutes in the preheated oven, until the chicken juices run clear, and cheese is melted and lightly browned.

Meatiest Vegetarian Chili from your Slow Cooker

Ingredients	Directions
❖ 1/2 cup olive oil ❖ 4 onions, chopped ❖ 2 green bell peppers, seeded and chopped ❖ 2 red bell peppers, seeded and chopped ❖ 4 cloves garlic, minced ❖ 1 (14 ounce) package firm tofu, drained and cubed ❖ 4 (15.5 ounce) cans black beans, drained ❖ 2 (15 ounce) cans crushed tomatoes ❖ 2 teaspoons salt ❖ 1/2 teaspoon ground black pepper ❖ 2 teaspoons ground cumin ❖ 6 tablespoons chili powder ❖ 2 tablespoons dried oregano ❖ 2 tablespoons distilled white vinegar ❖ 1 tablespoon liquid hot pepper sauce, such as Tabascoв„ў	Heat the olive oil in a large skillet over medium-high heat. Add the onions; cook and stir until they start to become soft. Add the green peppers, red peppers, garlic and tofu; cook and stir until vegetables are lightly browned and tender, the whole process should take about 10 minutes. Pour the black beans into the slow cooker and set to Low. Stir in the vegetables and tomatoes. Season with salt, pepper, cumin, chili powder, oregano, vinegar and hot pepper sauce. Stir gently and cover. Cook on LOW for 6 to 8 hours.

SwansonB® Black Bean, Corn and Turkey Chili

Ingredients	Directions
❖ 1 tablespoon vegetable oil ❖ 1 pound ground turkey ❖ 1 large onion, chopped ❖ 2 tablespoons chili powder ❖ 1 teaspoon ground cumin ❖ 1 teaspoon dried oregano leaves, crushed ❖ 1/2 teaspoon ground black pepper ❖ 1/4 teaspoon garlic powder ❖ 1 3/4 cups SwansonB® Chicken Broth (Regular, Natural GoodnessB„ÿ or Certified Organic) ❖ 1 cup PaceB® Thick & Chunky Salsa ❖ 1 tablespoon sugar ❖ 1 (15 ounce) can black beans, rinsed and drained ❖ 1 (16 ounce) can whole kernel corn, drained	Heat the oil in a 4-quart saucepot over medium-high heat. Add the turkey, onion, chili powder, cumin, oregano, black pepper and garlic powder. Cook until the turkey is well browned, stirring often. Stir the broth, salsa, sugar, beans and corn in the saucepot and heat to a boil. Reduce the heat to low. Cover and cook for 30 minutes or until the mixture is hot and bubbling.

Slow Cooker Chicken and Sausage Chili

Ingredients	Directions
❖ 3 (14.5 ounce) cans stewed tomatoes, chopped ❖ 1/2 cup beer ❖ 1/4 teaspoon hot sauce ❖ 2 beef bouillon cubes ❖ 1 tablespoon brown sugar ❖ 1/2 teaspoon chili powder ❖ 1/2 teaspoon paprika ❖ 1/4 teaspoon dried oregano ❖ 1/4 teaspoon garlic powder ❖ 1/8 teaspoon cayenne pepper ❖ 1 teaspoon olive oil ❖ 1/2 red onion, chopped	Combine the stewed tomatoes, beer, hot sauce, bouillon cubes, brown sugar, chili powder, paprika, oregano, garlic powder, and cayenne pepper in a slow cooker; cook on High for 1 hour. Heat the olive oil in a skillet over medium heat; cook the red onion in the hot oil until tender. Stir in the ground chicken; cook and stir until completely browned. Transfer the mixture to the slow cooker and return the skillet to the heat. Fry the

Ingredients	Directions
❖ 1 pound ground chicken ❖ 3/4 pound bulk Italian sausage ❖ 2 (6 ounce) cans tomato paste ❖ 1 (15 ounce) can kidney beans, rinsed and drained	sausage in the reheated skillet until completely browned and crumbly; add to the slow cooker. Mix the tomato paste and kidney beans into the chili. Continue cooking on High another 2 hours. Switch the heat to Low and simmer 4 hours more.

Campbell's® Slow Cooker Hearty Beef and Bean

Ingredients	Directions
❖ 1 1/2 pounds ground beef ❖ 1 large onion, chopped ❖ 2 cloves garlic, minced ❖ 1 (10.75 ounce) can Campbell's® Condensed Tomato Soup ❖ (Regular or 25% Less Sodium) ❖ 1 (14.5 ounce) can diced tomatoes ❖ 1/2 cup water ❖ 2 (15 ounce) cans kidney beans, rinsed and drained ❖ 1/4 cup chili powder ❖ 2 teaspoons ground cumin	Cook the beef in a 12-inch skillet over medium-high heat until it's well browned, stirring often. Pour off any fat. Stir the beef, onion, garlic, soup, tomatoes, water, beans, chili powder and cumin in a 3 1/2-quart slow cooker. Cover and cook on LOW for 8 to 9 hours.*

Italian Sausage Chili

Ingredients	Directions
❖ 1 celery rib, chopped ❖ 1 small onion, chopped ❖ 1/4 cup chopped green pepper ❖ 1/4 cup chopped sweet red pepper ❖ 1 tablespoon vegetable oil ❖ 1 Italian sausage link, casings removed ❖ 1 (14.5 ounce) can stewed tomatoes, undrained ❖ 1 cup canned kidney beans, rinsed and drained ❖ 1 cup water ❖ 5 tablespoons tomato paste ❖ 2 tablespoons chopped green chilies ❖ 3/4 teaspoon chili powder ❖ 1/4 teaspoon salt ❖ 1/4 teaspoon pepper ❖ 1/4 cup shredded Cheddar cheese	In a small saucepan, saute the celery, onion and sweet peppers in oil until crisp-tender. Crumble the sausage into a skillet; cook over medium heat until meat is no longer pink; drain. Stir in the tomatoes, kidney beans, water, tomato paste, chilies and seasonings; bring to a boil. Reduce heat; simmer, uncovered, for 20-30 minutes or until thickened. Sprinkle with cheese.

Quick and Spicy Chili

Ingredients	Directions
❖ 2 pounds lean ground beef ❖ 2 (15 ounce) cans kidney beans, drained and rinsed ❖ 1 (11 ounce) can whole kernel corn, drained ❖ 1 (15 ounce) can tomato sauce ❖ 1 (6 ounce) can tomato paste ❖ 2 cups water ❖ 2 jalapeno peppers ❖ 1 habanero pepper (optional) ❖ 1/2 red onion ❖ 2 large cloves garlic ❖ 3 tablespoons masa harina flour ❖ 1 tablespoon ground cayenne	Place the beef in a skillet over medium heat, and cook until evenly brown. Drain grease. In a large pot, mix the beans, corn, tomato sauce, tomato paste, and water. Bring to a boil, and reduce heat to low. In a food processor, finely chop the jalapenos, habanero, onion, and garlic. Mix into the pot. Mix in the cooked beef. Stir in masa flour. Season with cayenne pepper, chili powder, salt, black pepper, and sugar. Cook 45 minutes to 1 hour, stirring occasionally.

pepper ❖ 4 tablespoons chili powder ❖ 1 1/2 teaspoons salt ❖ 1 teaspoon ground black pepper ❖ 2 teaspoons white sugar (optional)	

Chili with Ground Pork

Ingredients	Directions
❖ 1 pound lean ground pork ❖ 2 tablespoons olive oil ❖ 4 medium onions, chopped ❖ 4 cloves garlic, minced ❖ 1 (8 ounce) can mushroom pieces ❖ 1 (14.5 ounce) can wax beans ❖ 1 (15 ounce) can sweet peas ❖ 1 green bell pepper, chopped ❖ 1 red bell pepper, chopped ❖ 1 (28 ounce) can tomato sauce chili powder to taste ❖ ground nutmeg to taste dried marjoram to taste salt to taste	Heat the olive oil in a large, deep skillet over medium heat, and cook the ground pork until evenly browned. Reserving the juices in the skillet, remove pork, and set aside. Stir the onions and garlic into the skillet, and cook in the pork juices over medium heat until tender. Mix in the mushrooms, wax beans, peas, green bell pepper, and red bell pepper. Cook and stir until tender and heated through. Return the pork to the skillet. Mix in the tomato sauce. Season with chili powder, nutmeg, marjoram, and salt. Reduce heat, and simmer about 45 minutes to allow the flavors to blend.

Tangy Chili

Ingredients	Directions
❖ 1 pound lean ground beef ❖ 1 (15 ounce) can sloppy joe sauce ❖ 1 (11 ounce) can whole kernel corn ❖ 1 (16 ounce) can chili beans in spicy sauce ❖ 1 (4.5 ounce) can sliced mushrooms	In a medium sized saute pan, brown ground beef and then drain fat. In a medium sauce pan combine browned beef, sloppy joe mix, corn, chili beans and mushrooms. Stir, heat through, and then serve.

Rapid Ragu® Chili

Ingredients	Directions
❖ 1 1/2 pounds lean ground beef ❖ 1 medium onion, chopped ❖ 2 tablespoons chili powder ❖ 1 (19 ounce) can kidney beans, rinsed and drained ❖ 1 (26 ounce) jar Ragu® Old World Style® Pasta Sauce ❖ 1 cup shredded Cheddar cheese	Brown ground beef with onion and chili powder in 12-inch skillet over medium-high heat, stirring occasionally. Stir in beans and Pasta Sauce. Bring to a boil over high heat. Reduce heat to low and simmer covered, stirring occasionally, 20 minutes. Top with cheese. Serve, if desired, over hot cooked rice or with tortilla chips.

Venison Burger and Steak Chili

Ingredients	Directions
❖ 1/2 pound bulk mild Italian sausage ❖ 1 pound cubed lean venison ❖ 2 pounds ground venison ❖ 2 tablespoons olive oil ❖ 8 ounces sliced crimini mushrooms ❖ 1 large onion, diced ❖ 2 tablespoons minced garlic ❖ 1 green pepper, diced ❖ 1 red peppers, diced ❖ 2 red chile peppers, seeded and chopped ❖ 2 jalapeno peppers, seeded and minced ❖ 1 (6 ounce) can tomato paste ❖ 1 (28 ounce) can tomato sauce ❖ 2 (15.5 ounce) cans black beans, rinsed and drained ❖ 2 (28 ounce) cans diced tomatoes, with liquid ❖ 1 cup water, or as needed ❖ 1/4 teaspoon chili powder	Cook sausage in a large skillet over medium-high heat until crumbled and browned; place into a large Dutch oven. Sear venison cubes until well browned; add to sausage. Add ground venison, and cook until crumbly and no longer pink; place into Dutch oven. Heat olive oil in the skillet over medium-high heat. Stir in the mushrooms, and cook until soft, about 2 minutes. Stir in onion and garlic, cook until the onion is translucent, about 2 minutes. Add the green and red peppers, red chile pepper, and jalapeno; cook until softened, then add to Dutch oven. Stir in tomato paste, tomato sauce, black beans, diced tomatoes, and water. Season with chili powder, paprika, cayenne, and oregano. Bring to a simmer over medium-high heat, then reduce heat to medium-low, cover, and simmer until the venison pieces are

Ingredients	Directions
❖ 2 tablespoons paprika ❖ 1 dash cayenne pepper ❖ 2 tablespoons dried oregano Salt and pepper to taste ❖ 1/4 cup minced fresh parsley ❖ 1 (8 ounce) package shredded Cheddar cheese	tender, about 2 hours. Season to taste with salt and pepper, and stir in parsley before serving. To serve, sprinkle with shredded Cheddar cheese.

Peanut Butter Chili

Ingredients	Directions
❖ 1 (14.5 ounce) can diced tomatoes ❖ 1/2 cup water ❖ 3 cloves garlic, minced ❖ 2 bay leaves ❖ 1/2 teaspoon cayenne pepper, or to taste ❖ 1 teaspoon chili powder ❖ 1 teaspoon garlic powder ❖ 1 teaspoon Italian seasoning ❖ 1 (15 ounce) can black beans, rinsed and drained ❖ 1 (15 ounce) can kidney beans, rinsed and drained ❖ 1/3 cup creamy peanut butter salt and pepper to taste ❖ 1 cup shredded Cheddar cheese (optional) ❖ 2 cups tortilla chips (optional)	Place the diced tomatoes, water, garlic, and bay leaves into a saucepan, and bring to a simmer over high heat. Reduce heat to medium-low, and season with the cayenne pepper, chili powder, garlic powder, and Italian seasoning. Cover, and simmer 15 minutes. After 15 minutes, pour in the black beans and kidney beans; return to a simmer, and cook for 5 minutes. Stir in the peanut butter until dissolved, then remove and discard the bay leaves, and season the chili with salt and pepper to taste. Enjoy with a sprinkle of Cheddar cheese, tortilla chips and smile!

White Chili I

Ingredients	Directions
❖ 1 pound ground pork ❖ 2 tablespoons olive oil ❖ 2 onions, chopped ❖ 5 cloves garlic, chopped ❖ 2 (4 ounce) cans diced green chiles ❖ 2 teaspoons ground cumin ❖ 1 teaspoon dried oregano ❖ 4 cups chicken broth ❖ 1 (14.5 ounce) can great Northern beans, rinsed and drained ❖ 2 cups shredded Monterey Jack cheese	Cook and drain the pork. In a large stockpot, saute onions and garlic in olive oil until transparent. Stir in the chilies, cumin, and oregano. Cook and stir 2 to 3 minutes more. Add broth, pork, and beans; bring to a boil. Reduce the heat to a simmer, and cook uncovered for 20 minutes. Remove from heat, and stir in the cheese until melted.

Delilah's Wicked Twelve Alarm Chili

Ingredients	Directions
❖ 1 (20 ounce) can kidney beans, undrained ❖ 2 (15 ounce) cans chili beans, undrained ❖ 2 (14 ounce) cans black beans, undrained ❖ 2 (15.5 ounce) cans black-eyed peas, undrained ❖ 1 (28 ounce) can diced tomatoes, undrained ❖ 2 pounds lean ground beef ❖ 1 pound hot Italian sausage ❖ 2 large green bell peppers, chopped ❖ 1 large red bell pepper, chopped ❖ 6 small yellow onions, chopped ❖ 1 red onion, chopped ❖ 6 cloves garlic, minced ❖ 1 (4 ounce) can sliced jalapeno peppers, finely chopped	Place the kidney beans, chili beans, black beans, and black-eyed peas in a large, heavy pot., and simmer over medium heat. Place the ground beef and sausage in a skillet over medium-high heat. Cook until crumbly and evenly browned, about 10 minutes. Drain, and stir into the bean mixture. Place the red and green bell peppers, yellow and red onions, and garlic on top of the bean and meat mixture. Cover and steam for at least 10 minutes. Stir in the jalapeno, chipotle, serrano, habanero, banana, cherry and Anaheim peppers, red and green Thai chilies, chili powder, cumin, red pepper flakes, and taco seasoning. Season to taste with cayenne pepper, salt, and black pepper. Cover,

Ingredients	Directions
❖ 1 (7 ounce) can chipotle chiles in adobo sauce, finely chopped ❖ 6 serrano peppers, finely chopped ❖ 4 orange habanero chili peppers, finely chopped ❖ 1 banana pepper, seeded and finely chopped ❖ 3 cherry peppers, finely chopped ❖ 1 Anaheim pepper, finely chopped ❖ 4 red Thai chili peppers, finely chopped ❖ 4 green Thai chili peppers, finely chopped ❖ 2 tablespoons chili powder, or to taste ❖ 1 1/2 tablespoons ground cumin ❖ 3 tablespoons red pepper flakes ❖ 1/3 envelope taco seasoning mix cayenne pepper, or amount to taste	and simmer over medium heat, stirring occasionally, for 3 hours.

Green Chili Casserole

Ingredients	Directions
❖ 1 pound ground beef ❖ 8 (6 inch) corn tortillas ❖ 1 small onion, diced ❖ 1 pound processed cheese food, shredded ❖ 1 (4 ounce) can green chile peppers, chopped ❖ 1 (10.75 ounce) can condensed cream of chicken soup ❖ 1/2 cup milk	Preheat oven to 325 degrees F (165 degrees C). Grease a medium sized casserole dish. In a medium skillet over medium heat, cook the ground beef until evenly browned; drain fat. Place half of the tortillas on the bottom of the prepared casserole dish and spread with half of the onion, cheese, ground beef and chiles. Layer with the remaining tortillas, onion, half of the remaining cheese, ground beef and chiles. In a medium bowl, dilute the soup with milk and pour over the top of the casserole.

	Bake in the preheated oven for 30 minutes. Sprinkle with the remaining cheese and bake for another 5 to 10 minutes, or until the cheese has melted.

Waistline-Friendly Turkey Chili

Ingredients	Directions
❖ 1 pound ground turkey ❖ 1/2 cup diced onion ❖ 1 clove garlic, minced ❖ 1/2 cup diced green bell pepper ❖ 1/2 cup diced red bell pepper ❖ 1 (14.5 ounce) can diced tomatoes ❖ 1 cup medium salsa ❖ 1 cup chipotle barbeque sauce ❖ 1 (4 ounce) can chopped green chilies ❖ 1 cup corn kernels ❖ 1 (15 ounce) can black beans, rinsed and drained ❖ 1 tablespoon lime juice ❖ 1 teaspoon ground cumin ❖ 1 tablespoon crushed red pepper flakes ❖ 1 tablespoon chili powder ❖ 1 tablespoon dried cilantro ❖ 1/2 teaspoon salt ❖ 1 cup fat-free sour cream, for garnish (optional)	Heat a large, nonstick pot over medium-high heat and stir in the ground turkey, onion, garlic, green pepper, and red pepper. Cook and stir until the turkey is crumbly, evenly browned, and no longer pink, about 10 minutes. Pour in the tomatoes, salsa, barbeque sauce, green chiles, corn, and black beans. Season with lime juice, cumin, red pepper flakes, chili powder, and cilantro. Bring to a simmer over medium-high heat, then reduce heat to medium-low, cover, and simmer until the flavors develop, 1 to 3 hours. Serve with a dollop of sour cream on each serving.

Chicken Skewers with Thai Chili Sauce

Ingredients	Directions
❖ 1 1/2 pounds ground chicken ❖ 1/4 cup finely chopped fresh cilantro ❖ 1/3 cup VH® Sweet Thai Chili Sauce (plus extra for pitas) 1/2 cup dry bread crumbs ❖ 1 egg ❖ 2 tablespoons VH® Soya Sauce ❖ 8 wooden skewers, soaked in water for 20 minutes ❖ Pita bread, shredded lettuce, diced tomato and slivered onion for garnishing	Mix together the chicken, cilantro, VH® Sweet Thai Chili Sauce, bread crumbs, egg and VH® Soya Sauce until well combined. With wet hands form 8 equal portions onto skewers and form into a sausage-like shape, covering the pointed end of skewer. Roast skewers on a foil lined baking sheet in a 500 degrees F (260 degrees C) oven for 20 minutes or until cooked through. Serve with additional chili sauce for dipping or serve in warmed pita bread garnished with shredded lettuce, diced tomato and slivered onion.

Tommy's Chili

Ingredients	Directions
❖ 1 pound ground beef ❖ 1 1/2 cups all-purpose flour, divided ❖ 1 1/3 cups beef broth ❖ 1 quart water ❖ 3 tablespoons chili powder ❖ 2 tablespoons finely grated carrot ❖ 1 tablespoon white vinegar ❖ 2 teaspoons dried minced onion ❖ 2 teaspoons salt ❖ 1 teaspoon granulated sugar ❖ 1 teaspoon paprika ❖ 1/4 teaspoon garlic powder	Place the beef in a large, deep skillet over medium heat, and cook until evenly brown. Transfer beef to a strainer over a saucepan, and allow grease to drain for about 5 minutes. Mix any drippings remaining in skillet into the saucepan. There should be about 1/2 cup drippings. Return beef to skillet. Heat the beef drippings in the saucepan over medium heat, and gradually mix in 1/4 cup flour. Reduce heat to low, and continue cooking 10 minutes, stirring continuously, to form a golden brown roux. Pour in the beef broth, and remove from heat.

	Pour the water into the skillet with the beef, and mix in remaining flour. Stir in the roux mixture, chili powder, carrot, vinegar, onion, salt, sugar, paprika, and garlic powder. Bring to a boil, reduce heat to medium-low, and continue cooking 15 minutes, until thickened. When it's done cooking, take the chili off the heat, cover it, and let it sit for 30 minutes before using it on burgers, etc. It should thicken to a tasty brown paste as it sits.

Chili Bean Cheese Omelet

Ingredients	Directions
❖ 1/2 cup chopped fresh tomato ❖ 1 green onion, chopped ❖ 1/4 cup canned kidney beans, coarsely chopped ❖ 1 garlic clove, minced ❖ 1/8 teaspoon celery salt ❖ 1/8 teaspoon chili powder ❖ 1/8 teaspoon Worcestershire sauce ❖ 2 teaspoons vegetable oil, divided ❖ 2 eggs ❖ 1/4 teaspoon salt ❖ 1/4 cup shredded mozzarella cheese	In a skillet, saute the tomato, onion, beans, garlic, celery salt, chili powder and Worcestershire sauce in 1 teaspoon oil until liquid has evaporated; set aside and keep warm. In a bowl, beat eggs and salt. Heat remaining oil in an 8-in. skillet over medium-low heat; add eggs. As eggs set, lift edges, letting uncooked portion flow underneath. When the eggs are nearly set, sprinkle vegetable mixture over one side. Fold omelet over filling. Sprinkle with cheese. Cover and let stand for 1-2 minutes or until cheese is melted.

Fairuzah's Chili

Ingredients	Directions
❖ 1 1/2 pounds ground beef ❖ 1 1/2 pounds ground turkey ❖ 3/4 large white onion, diced ❖ 3 (15 ounce) cans kidney beans, drained ❖ 3 (15 ounce) cans baked beans with pork ❖ 1 (14.5 ounce) can stewed tomatoes ❖ 1 (12 ounce) can sliced mushrooms, drained ❖ 3 tablespoons chili powder ❖ 6 cloves garlic, minced ❖ 1 1/2 teaspoons garlic powder ❖ 1 teaspoon ground cinnamon salt and pepper to taste	In a large pot, combine the ground beef, ground turkey, and onion. Cook, stirring, over medium heat until meat is cooked through, about 10 minutes. Stir in the kidney beans, baked beans, tomatoes, and mushrooms. Season with chili powder, garlic, garlic powder, cinnamon, salt, and pepper. Reduce heat to low, and simmer for at least 1 hour, stirring occasionally. The longer the better. After the first half-hour has passed, taste, and adjust seasonings to suit your preference.

Slow-Cooked Habanero Chili

Ingredients	Directions
❖ 3 tablespoons olive oil ❖ 1 pound lean ground turkey ❖ 1 cup red bell pepper, chopped ❖ 3 cloves garlic, minced ❖ 1 (16 ounce) can kidney beans, rinsed and drained ❖ 1 (16 ounce) can black beans, rinsed and drained ❖ 1 cup rinsed and drained canned black-eyed peas ❖ 1 (15 ounce) can low sodium tomato sauce ❖ 1 dried habanero pepper, chopped ❖ 1 cup frozen corn kernels ❖ 1 tablespoon packed brown sugar ❖ 1 teaspoon Worcestershire sauce	Heat 1 tablespoon of olive oil in a large skillet over medium-high heat. Add the ground turkey and cook until no longer pink and evenly browned, about 10 minutes. Using a slotted spoon, place the cooked meat into a slow cooker, and drain any oil from the skillet. Using the same skillet, heat the remaining 2 tablespoons of olive oil over medium-high heat. Stir in the red pepper and garlic; cook until tender, about 3 minutes. Stir into the slow cooker with the turkey. Stir the kidney beans, black beans, black-eyed peas, tomato sauce, and habanero pepper into the slow cooker with the

❖ 1 tablespoon dried basil ❖ 1 teaspoon dried sage salt to taste	turkey and onion mixture. Set on High and cook for 3 hours or on Low for 7 hours. One hour before the time is up, stir in the corn, brown sugar, Worcestershire sauce, basil, and sage. Continue cooking the chili for the remaining hour. Season to taste with salt.

Chili-Topped Taters

Ingredients	Directions
❖ 6 large potatoes ❖ 2 pounds ground beef ❖ 1 medium onion, chopped ❖ 1 (16 ounce) can kidney beans, rinsed and drained ❖ 1 (16 ounce) can pork and beans, undrained ❖ 1 (15 ounce) can tomato sauce ❖ 2 tablespoons chili powder ❖ 1 tablespoon dried parsley flakes ❖ 1 teaspoon dried oregano ❖ 1/2 teaspoon garlic powder salt and pepper to taste ❖ 3/4 cup shredded Cheddar cheese	Scrub and pierce potatoes. Bake at 375* degrees Ffor 1 hour or until tender. Meanwhile, in a large saucepan, cook beef and onion over medium heat until meat is no longer pink; drain. Add beans, tomato sauce and seasonings; mix well. Bring to a boil. Reduce heat; simmer, uncovered, for 30 minutes. When potatoes are cool enough to handle, cut an X in the top of each with a sharp knife. Fluff pulp with a fork; top with chili and cheese

Hoosier Chili

Ingredients	Directions
❖ 2 pounds extra-lean ground beef ❖ 2 cups chopped onion ❖ 3/4 cup chopped celery ❖ 1/2 cup chopped green pepper ❖ 3 garlic cloves, minced ❖ 1 teaspoon salt ❖ 1/4 teaspoon pepper ❖ 1 tablespoon brown sugar ❖ 3 tablespoons chili powder ❖ 2 (16 ounce) cans stewed tomatoes ❖ 1 (46 ounce) can tomato juice ❖ 1 (10.5 ounce) can beef broth ❖ 1/2 cup uncooked elbow ❖ macaroni ❖ 1 (15 ounce) can kidney beans, rinsed and drained	In a large Dutch oven or soup kettle, brown beef until no longer pink. Add onion, celery, green pepper and garlic. Continue cooking until vegetables are tender. Add all remaining ingredients except last two; bring to a boil. Reduce heat; cover and simmer for 1-1/2 hours, adding macaroni for last half hour of cooking time. Stir in the beans and heat through.

Quick and Easy Chili Dip

Ingredients	Directions
❖ 2 (15 ounce) cans chili with beans ❖ 2 (8 ounce) packages cream cheese, softened ❖ 1 cup chunky salsa ❖ 1 (13 ounce) can roast beef, shredded ❖ 1 (14.5 ounce) package tortilla chips	Place chili, cream cheese, salsa, and roast beef in a large saucepan. Heat slowly, stirring occasionally until the mixture comes to a slow boil. Serve with chips and enjoy!

Chili-Crusted Tri-Tip Roast

Ingredients	Directions
❖ 1 (1 1/2 pound) beef tri-tip roast Salt and pepper Rub: ❖ 1 tablespoon chili powder ❖ 2 teaspoons ground cumin ❖ 1 teaspoon onion powder ❖ 1/2 teaspoon garlic powder ❖ 1/4 teaspoon pepper	Heat oven to 425 degrees F. Combine rub ingredients in small bowl; press evenly onto all surfaces of beef roast. Place roast on rack in shallow roasting pan. Do not add water or cover. Roast in 425 degrees F oven 30 to 40 minutes for medium rare; 40 to 45 minutes for medium doneness. Remove roast when instant-read thermometer registers 135 degrees F for medium rare; 150 degrees F for medium. Transfer roast to carving board; tent loosely with aluminum foil. Let stand 15 minutes. (Temperature will continue to rise about 10 degrees F to reach 145 degrees F for medium rare; 160 degrees F for medium.) Carve roast across the grain into thin slices. Season with salt and pepper, as desired.

Black Bean Chili

Ingredients	Directions
❖ 1 tablespoon olive oil ❖ 1 onion, chopped ❖ 2 red bell pepper, seeded and chopped ❖ 1 jalapeno pepper, seeded and minced ❖ 10 fresh mushrooms, quartered ❖ 6 roma (plum) tomatoes, diced ❖ 1 cup fresh corn kernels ❖ 1 teaspoon ground black pepper ❖ 1 teaspoon ground cumin	Heat oil in a large saucepan over medium-high heat. Sautee the onion, red bell peppers, jalapeno, mushrooms, tomatoes and corn for 10 minutes or until the onions are translucent. Season with black pepper, cumin and chili powder. Stir in the black beans, chicken broth and salt. Bring to a boil. Remove 1 1/2 cups of the soup to food processor or blender; puree and stir the

❖ 1 tablespoon chili powder ❖ 2 (15 ounce) cans black beans, drained and rinsed ❖ 1 1/2 cups chicken broth ❖ 1 teaspoon salt	bean mixture back into the soup. Serve hot by itself or over rice.

No Tomato Chili

Ingredients	Directions
❖ 2 1/2 pounds lean ground beef salt to taste ❖ 1 medium onion, chopped ❖ 1 green bell pepper, seeded and chopped (optional) ❖ 3 cloves garlic, pressed ❖ 1/4 cup Worcestershire sauce ❖ 5 tablespoons chili powder ❖ 2 teaspoons ground cumin ❖ 2 teaspoons dried oregano ❖ 1 (15 ounce) can kidney beans, rinsed and drained ❖ 1 (15 ounce) can cannellini beans, rinsed and drained ❖ 2 (12 ounce) bottles chile sauce ❖ 1 (14 ounce) can beef broth ❖ 2 cups shredded Cheddar cheese 1/4 cup chopped jalapeno pepper (optional)	Crumble the ground beef into a soup pot over medium-high heat. Cook and stir until browned. Drain off the grease, and season with salt to taste. Add the onion, bell pepper, and garlic; cook and stir for about 3 minutes. Reduce the heat to medium, and season with Worcestershire sauce, chili powder, cumin and oregano. Cook and stir for another 5 minutes. Reduce heat to low, and stir in the chili sauce, beef broth, kidney beans and cannellini beans. Cover, and simmer for about 35 minutes. Ladle into bowls to serve, and top with shredded Cheddar cheese and jalapeno

Thai Chili Butter Sauce

Ingredients	Directions
❖ 1 tablespoon Thai chili-garlic sauce ❖ 1/2 tablespoon minced garlic ❖ 3 tablespoons fresh lime juice ❖ 1/3 cup white wine ❖ 1/2 cup heavy cream ❖ 1/2 cup unsalted butter, softened salt and ground black pepper to taste	Stir the chili-garlic sauce, garlic, lime juice, and white wine together in a small saucepan over medium-high heat; allow the mixture to simmer until reduced to about 1/3 its original volume, about 10 minutes. Set aside to cool. Pour the heavy cream into a saucepan and cook over medium heat until reduced to about 1/3 its original volume, about 10 minutes. Reduce heat the medium low. Whisk the cooled garlic mixture into the cream. Add the butter to the mixture about 2 tablespoons at a time, whisking vigorously to incorporate. Season with salt and pepper to serve.

Veggie Vegetarian Chili

Ingredients	Directions
❖ 1 tablespoon vegetable oil ❖ 3 cloves garlic, minced ❖ 1 cup chopped onion ❖ 1 cup chopped carrots ❖ 1 cup chopped green bell pepper ❖ 1 cup chopped red bell pepper ❖ 2 tablespoons chili powder ❖ 1 1/2 cups chopped fresh mushrooms ❖ 1 (28 ounce) can whole peeled tomatoes with liquid, chopped ❖ 1 (15 ounce) can black beans, undrained ❖ 1 (15 ounce) can kidney beans, undrained ❖ 1 (15 ounce) can pinto beans, undrained	Heat the oil in a large pot over medium heat. Cook and stir the garlic, onion, and carrots in the pot until tender. Mix in the green bell pepper and red bell pepper. Season with chili powder. Continue cooking 5 minutes, or until peppers are tender. Mix the mushrooms into the pot. Stir in the tomatoes with liquid, black beans with liquid, kidney beans with liquid, pinto beans with liquid, and corn. Season with cumin, oregano, basil, and garlic powder. Bring to a boil. Reduce heat to medium, cover, and cook 20 minutes, stirring occasionally.

Ingredients	Directions
❖ 1 (15 ounce) can whole kernel corn, drained ❖ 1 tablespoon cumin ❖ 1 1/2 tablespoons dried oregano ❖ 1 1/2 tablespoons dried basil ❖ 1/2 tablespoon garlic powder	

Killer Chili

Ingredients	Directions
❖ 1 (1 pound) package bacon ❖ 3 pounds ground beef ❖ 4 cloves garlic, minced ❖ 2 cups red wine ❖ 3 (28 ounce) cans diced tomatoes ❖ 2 (14 ounce) cans tomato sauce ❖ 2 teaspoons vegetable oil ❖ 3 green bell peppers, chopped ❖ 4 stalks celery, chopped ❖ 2 onions, chopped ❖ 2 (19 ounce) cans kidney beans, rinsed and drained ❖ 2 (19 ounce) cans white beans, rinsed and drained ❖ 1 (19 ounce) can black beans, rinsed and drained ❖ 6 tablespoons chili powder ❖ 1/4 cup brown sugar ❖ 1/4 cup ground cumin ❖ 3 tablespoons paprika ❖ 2 tablespoons Italian seasoning ❖ 2 tablespoons distilled white vinegar ❖ 2 tablespoons dried basil ❖ 2 tablespoons dried minced onion ❖ 3 tablespoons dried parsley ❖ 2 tablespoons crushed red pepper flakes ❖ 4 teaspoons dried oregano ❖ 12 dashes hot pepper sauce (such as Tabasco®)	Place the bacon in a large, deep skillet, and cook over medium-high heat, turning occasionally, until evenly browned, about 10 minutes. Drain the bacon slices on a paper towel-lined plate. Crumble and set aside. Heat a large stock pot over medium-high heat and cook and stir the ground beef until the beef is crumbly, evenly browned, and no longer pink. Drain and discard any excess grease. Stir in the bacon and minced garlic. Reduce heat to medium-low and stir in the red wine, diced tomatoes, and tomato sauce. Heat the vegetable oil in a skillet over medium heat. Stir in the green bell peppers, celery, and chopped onion; cook and stir until the onion has softened and turned translucent, about 5 minutes. Stir onion mixture into the stock pot. Increase the heat to medium-high and bring to a near boil. Mix in the kidney beans, white beans, and black beans. Season with chili powder, brown sugar, cumin, paprika, Italian seasoning, vinegar, basil, dried minced onion, parsley, red pepper flakes, oregano, hot pepper sauce, salt, and pepper. Reduce heat to medium-low and simmer for 1 hour 30 minutes, stirring often

❖ salt and ground black pepper to taste (optional)	

Terrific Turkey Chili

Ingredients	Directions
❖ 3 tablespoons vegetable oil, divided ❖ 1 1/2 pounds ground turkey ❖ 1 (1 ounce) package taco seasoning mix ❖ 1 teaspoon ground coriander ❖ 1 teaspoon dried oregano ❖ 1 teaspoon chili pepper flakes ❖ 2 tablespoons tomato paste ❖ 1 (14.5 ounce) can beef broth ❖ 1 (7 ounce) can salsa ❖ 1 (14.5 ounce) can crushed tomatoes, or coarsely chopped tomatoes packed in puree ❖ 1 (7 ounce) can chopped green chile peppers ❖ 1 medium onion, finely chopped ❖ 1 green bell pepper, diced ❖ 3 medium zucchini, halved lengthwise and sliced ❖ 1 bunch green onions, chopped ❖ 1 cup sour cream ❖ 1 cup shredded Cheddar cheese	Heat 1 tablespoon of oil in a large stock pot over medium-high heat. Crumble turkey into the pot, stirring with a wooden spoon to break apart as much as possible. Season with taco seasoning mix, coriander, oregano, chili flakes, and tomato paste, and mix until meat is evenly coated with seasonings. Continue cooking, reducing heat if necessary, until turkey is well browned. Pour in beef broth, and simmer to reduce liquid slightly, about 5 minutes. Add salsa, tomatoes, and green chilies, and continue cooking at a moderate simmer for ten minutes. Adjust the thickness at any time you feel necessary by adding water. While chili is still cooking, heat one tablespoon of oil in a large skillet over medium-high heat. Cook onion and green bell pepper, stirring occasionally for 5 minutes, or until onion is translucent and bell pepper is lightly browned. Add onion and bell pepper to the chili, and continue cooking at a very low simmer. In the same skillet, heat the remaining tablespoon of oil over medium-high heat. Add the zucchini, and cook stirring occasionally, for 5 minutes, or until lightly browned. Add the zucchini to the chili, reduce heat, and continue cooking 15 minutes more. Again, adjust the consistency with water as needed.

	Ladle chili into serving bowls. Top with sour cream, green onion, and cheddar cheese, and serve.

Cheesy Taco Chili

Ingredients	Directions
❖ 1 1/2 pounds ground beef ❖ 1/2 cup chopped onion ❖ 1 pound process cheese (eg. Velveeta), cubed ❖ 1 (16 ounce) jar salsa ❖ 1 (16 ounce) can red beans, drained and rinsed ❖ 1 (14.5 ounce) can stewed tomatoes, undrained ❖ 1 (10 ounce) can diced tomatoes and green chilies, undrained ❖ 1/2 teaspoon chili powder ❖ 1 cup sour cream	In a large saucepan or Dutch oven, cook beef and onion over medium heat until meat is no longer pink; drain. Stir in the cheese, salsa, beans, tomatoes and chili powder. Cook for 10 minutes or until cheese is melted. Remove from the heat; stir in sour cream.

Wicked Good Veggie Chili

Ingredients	Directions
❖ 1/2 cup texturized vegetable protein (TVP) ❖ 1 cup water ❖ 2 1/2 tablespoons olive oil ❖ 1 onion, chopped ❖ 6 cloves garlic, minced ❖ 1 teaspoon salt ❖ 1 teaspoon ground black pepper ❖ 2 teaspoons chili powder ❖ 2 teaspoons ground cumin ❖ 2 teaspoons ground cayenne pepper ❖ 1/4 teaspoon cinnamon ❖ 1 tablespoon honey ❖ 2 (12 ounce) cans kidney beans with liquid	Place the textured vegetable protein (TVP) in water, and soak 30 minutes. Press to drain. Heat the oil in a large pot over medium heat, and saute TVP, onion, and garlic until onion is tender and TVP is evenly browned. Season with salt, pepper, 1/2 the chili powder, 1/2 the cumin, 1/2 the cayenne pepper, and cinnamon. Mix in honey, beans, tomatoes, green bell pepper, and carrots. Cook, stirring, occasionally, 45 minutes. Season the chili with remaining chili powder, cumin, and cayenne pepper,

Ingredients	Directions
❖ 2 (12 ounce) cans diced tomatoes with juice ❖ 1 green bell pepper, chopped ❖ 2 carrots, finely chopped ❖ 1 bunch green onions, chopped ❖ 1 bunch cilantro, chopped ❖ 1 (8 ounce) container dairy sour cream	and continue cooking 15 minutes. To serve, divide into bowls, garnish with green onions and cilantro, and top with dollops of sour cream.

Lentil Chili

Ingredients	Directions
❖ 2 tablespoons vegetable oil ❖ 1 onion, chopped ❖ 4 cloves garlic, minced ❖ 1 cup dry lentils ❖ 1 cup dry bulgur wheat ❖ 3 cups low fat, low sodium chicken broth ❖ 2 cups canned whole tomatoes, chopped ❖ 2 tablespoons chili powder ❖ 1 tablespoon ground cumin salt and pepper to taste	In a large pot over medium high heat, combine the oil, onion and garlic and saute for 5 minutes. Stir in the lentils and bulgur wheat. Add the broth, tomatoes, chili powder, cumin and salt and pepper to taste. Bring to a boil, reduce heat to low and simmer for 30 minutes, or until lentils are tender.

Chili Verde

Ingredients	Directions
❖ 3 tablespoons Worcestershire sauce ❖ 1 tablespoon garlic pepper ❖ 3 pounds pork picnic roast ❖ 1 large onion, diced ❖ 1 (14.5 ounce) can chicken broth ❖ 2 (4 ounce) cans diced green chilies, drained ❖ 3 (7 ounce) cans green salsa	Pour half of the Worcestershire sauce into the pan of a slow cooker, and half of the garlic pepper. Place the roast in the pan, and sprinkle remaining Worcestershire sauce and garlic pepper over the top. Add the onions, and chilies, and pour in the chicken broth. Cover, and cook on Low for 8 to 10 hours. When the roast is tender enough to pull

	apart with a fork, add the green salsa, and the beans, if desired. Continue cooking until heated through. Serve as soup or over chimichangas.
❖ 2 (15.5 ounce) cans great Northern beans, drained (optional)	

Chicken Chili II

Ingredients	Directions
❖ 1 pound skinless, boneless chicken breast meat - finely chopped ❖ 4 tablespoons olive oil ❖ 1 onion, finely diced ❖ 3 cloves garlic, minced ❖ 1 red bell pepper, diced ❖ 1 yellow bell pepper, chopped ❖ 1 tablespoon chili powder ❖ 1 teaspoon ground cumin ❖ 1 teaspoon dried oregano ❖ 5 cups chicken broth ❖ 2 (15 ounce) cans cannellini beans ❖ 1 (4 ounce) can diced green chiles ❖ 1/4 cup cornmeal (optional) ❖ salt and pepper to taste 1/4 teaspoon hot pepper sauce	In a large stock pot, saute chicken, olive oil, onion, garlic, red bell pepper and yellow bell pepper, until vegetables start to soften. Add chili powder, cumin and oregano. Cook on medium for 3 minutes. Add chicken broth, beans and green chilies and continue to cook on medium low for 5 to 10 minutes. If you want to thicken soup, mix cornmeal with a little water to form a paste and add to chili. Season with salt, pepper and hot sauce and serve.

Russian Chili

Ingredients	Directions
❖ 2 pounds ground beef ❖ 1 tablespoon olive oil ❖ 2 onions, chopped ❖ 1 green bell pepper, chopped ❖ 2 stalks celery, chopped ❖ 1 (12 fluid ounce) can or bottle flat beer ❖ 1 cup water ❖ 2 tablespoons chili powder salt and pepper to taste ❖ 1/2 teaspoon dried parsley ❖ 1 teaspoon ground cumin ❖ 1 (6 ounce) can tomato paste ❖ 1 (15 ounce) can kidney beans ❖ 1 cup sour cream	In a large skillet over medium heat, cook beef until brown. Drain and let cool. Rinse with water. Drain. In a large pot over medium heat, cook onion, bell pepper and celery in oil until just tender. Stir in ground beef, beer, water, chili powder, salt, pepper, parsley and cumin. Reduce heat, cover and simmer 30 minutes. Stir in tomato paste and cook 10 minutes more. Stir in kidney beans and heat through. Remove from heat and stir in sour cream.

Black Bean Chili

Ingredients	Directions
❖ 2 cups chopped sweet onions ❖ 2 tablespoons canola oil ❖ 1/2 pound fresh mushrooms, sliced ❖ 1 large green pepper, chopped ❖ 1 large sweet yellow pepper, chopped ❖ 1 large sweet red pepper, chopped ❖ 3 garlic cloves, minced ❖ 2 (15 ounce) cans black beans, rinsed and drained ❖ 2 (14.5 ounce) cans diced tomatoes, undrained ❖ 1 (15 ounce) can tomato sauce ❖ 1 (6 ounce) can tomato paste ❖ 2 tablespoons brown sugar ❖ 2 teaspoons chili powder	In a Dutch oven or soup kettle, saute onions in oil for 5 minutes. Add mushrooms, peppers and garlic; saute for 5-6 minutes or until vegetables are tender. Stir in the remaining ingredients; bring to a boil. Reduce heat; cover and simmer for 20-25 minutes or until heated through.

❖ 2 teaspoons ground cumin ❖ 1 dash hot pepper sauce	

Chili Bean Dip

Ingredients	Directions
❖ 1 (15 ounce) can chili with beans ❖ 1 (8 ounce) package cream cheese, softened ❖ 1/2 (8 ounce) package cream cheese with chives ❖ 1/2 cup shredded Cheddar cheese	In a medium saucepan over medium low heat, mix together chili with beans, cream cheese, cream cheese with chives and Cheddar cheese. Stirring often, heat until melted and well blended, about 20 minutes.

Chicken and Two Bean Chili

Ingredients	Directions
❖ 2 chicken breasts, cut into chunks ❖ 1 tablespoon olive oil ❖ 1/3 red onion, chopped ❖ 3 cloves garlic, minced ❖ 1 (15 ounce) can black beans, drained ❖ 1 (14.5 ounce) can great Northern beans, drained ❖ 2 (14.5 ounce) cans diced ❖ tomatoes with green chile peppers ❖ 1 (14 ounce) can tomato sauce ❖ 1/2 cup chicken stock ❖ 1/2 cup brown sugar ❖ 1/2 cup frozen corn ❖ 1/4 cup white vinegar ❖ 3 tablespoons chili powder ❖ 3 tablespoons ground cumin ❖ 2 tablespoons dried cilantro Dash of salt ❖ 1 pinch cayenne pepper	Fill a large pot with lightly-salted water and bring to a boil. Boil the chicken until no longer pink in the center and the juices run clear, 7 to 10 minutes. Drain the chicken and place in a slow cooker. Heat the olive oil in a skillet over medium heat. Brown the onion and garlic in the hot oil, 5 to 7 minutes; scrape into the slow cooker. Add the black beans, great Northern beans, tomatoes with green chiles, tomato sauce, chicken stock, brown sugar, corn, vinegar, chili powder, cumin, cilantro, salt, and cayenne pepper to the slow cooker. Cook on High until the beans are tender, 3 to 4 hours. Stir the diced green, red, and yellow bell peppers into the chili and cook another 20 minutes.

❖ 1/2 green bell peppers, diced ❖ 1/2 red bell pepper, diced ❖ 1/2 yellow bell pepper, diced	

BBQ Chili Pasta

Ingredients	Directions
❖ 1 (8 ounce) package rotini pasta ❖ 1 tablespoon olive oil ❖ 1 onion, chopped ❖ 8 ounces ground turkey ❖ 1 green bell pepper, chopped ❖ 1 (15 ounce) can whole kernel corn, drained ❖ 1 tablespoon chili powder ❖ 1 tablespoon dried oregano ❖ 1/2 teaspoon salt ❖ 1 (8 ounce) can tomato sauce ❖ 3/4 cup barbecue sauce	In a large pot with boiling salted water cook rotelle pasta until al dente. Drain. Meanwhile, in a large non-stick skillet heat oil over medium-high heat, add onion and cook until onion for 2 minutes, or until softened. Add ground turkey and cook until no pink remains, about 3 to 4 minutes. Stir in chopped green bell pepper, corn, chili powder, dried oregano, salt, tomato sauce, and BBQ sauce. Bring mixture to a boil. Reduce heat to medium and simmer until slightly thickened, about 3 to 4 minutes, stirring occasionally. In a large serving bowl, combine the turkey mixture with the pasta. Serve immediately.

Chili Noodle Casserole

Ingredients	Directions
❖ 12 ounces spaghetti ❖ 1 pound lean ground beef ❖ 1 onion, chopped ❖ salt and pepper to taste chili powder to taste ❖ 1 (15.25 ounce) can kidney beans, drained	Bring a large pot of lightly salted water to a boil. Add pasta and cook for 8 to 10 minutes or until al dente; drain. Meanwhile, brown the meat with the onion ina skillet; drain off liquids. Stir in salt, pepper, and chili powder to taste. Stir in kidney beans, and saute 5 to 10 minutes. Serve meat and bean mixture over pasta.

Green Chili and Corn Dip

Ingredients	Directions
❖ 1 1/2 cups whole peeled tomatoes, drained and chopped ❖ 1/4 cup whole kernel corn, drained ❖ 1/4 cup milk ❖ 1/4 cup all-purpose flour ❖ 1 (16 ounce) package shredded Cheddar cheese ❖ 1 (4 ounce) can chopped green chile peppers	In a medium saucepan over medium heat, mix tomatoes, corn, milk and flour. Cook and stir until thick and bubbly, about 10 minutes. Gradually blend in Cheddar cheese and diced green chile peppers. Continue cooking until cheese has melted, about 10 minutes. Serve warm.

Camp Chili

Ingredients	Directions
❖ 3 pounds ground beef ❖ 3 onions, chopped ❖ 10 cloves garlic, minced ❖ 3 (15 ounce) cans pork and beans ❖ 3 (15 ounce) cans kidney beans ❖ 1 (14.5 ounce) can stewed tomatoes ❖ 3 tablespoons chili powder ❖ 1 (12 fluid ounce) can or bottle beer ❖ salt and pepper to taste ❖ 3 cups uncooked rice	In a large pot over medium high heat, saute the ground beef for 5 minutes. Add the onions and garlic and saute for 5 to 10 more minutes. Add the pork and beans, kidney beans, tomatoes, chili powder, beer and season with salt and pepper to taste. Stir thoroughly and reduce heat to medium low. Cover and simmer for 1 to 1 1/2 hours, stirring occasionally. Cook the rice according to package directions. Serve the chili over the rice.

Chili-ghetti

Ingredients	Directions
❖ 1 (7 ounce) package spaghetti ❖ 1 pound ground beef ❖ 1 small onion, chopped ❖ 1 (16 ounce) can kidney beans, rinsed and drained ❖ 1 (14.5 ounce) can diced tomatoes, undrained ❖ 1 (4 ounce) can mushroom stems and pieces, drained ❖ 1/3 cup water ❖ 1 (1.25 ounce) package chili seasoning mix ❖ 2 tablespoons grated Parmesan cheese ❖ 1/4 cup shredded mozzarella cheese	Cook spaghetti according to package directions. Meanwhile, in a large skillet, cook beef and onion over medium heat until meat is no longer pink; drain. Drain spaghetti; add to beef mixture. Stir in the beans, tomatoes, mushrooms, water, chili seasoning and Parmesan cheese. Cover and simmer for 10 minutes. Sprinkle with mozzarella cheese.

No Beans About It - Chili

Ingredients	Directions
❖ 1 pound ground beef ❖ 2 cloves garlic, minced ❖ 1 large onion, chopped ❖ 2 tablespoons chili powder ❖ 1 teaspoon dried oregano ❖ 1 teaspoon ground cumin ❖ 1 teaspoon hot pepper sauce ❖ 1 (28 ounce) can crushed tomatoes ❖ 1/4 cup red wine vinegar	Crumble the ground beef into a stock pot or large Dutch oven over medium-high heat. Add the onion and garlic, and cook stirring frequently until beef is evenly browned. Drain off excess grease. Season with chili powder, oregano, cumin and hot sauce. Stir in the tomatoes and vinegar. Bring to a boil, then reduce heat to low, and simmer for about 1 hour - or longer if you have time. Stir occasionally to prevent burning on the bottom.

White Chili I

Ingredients	Directions
❖ 1 tablespoon olive oil ❖ 4 skinless, boneless chicken breast halves - cubed ❖ 1 onion, chopped ❖ 1 1/4 cups chicken broth ❖ 1 (4 ounce) can diced green chiles ❖ 1 teaspoon garlic powder ❖ 1 teaspoon ground cumin ❖ 1/2 teaspoon dried oregano ❖ 1/2 teaspoon dried cilantro ❖ 1/8 teaspoon cayenne pepper ❖ 1 (15 ounce) can cannellini beans, drained and rinsed ❖ 2 green onions, chopped ❖ 2 ounces shredded Monterey Jack cheese	Heat oil in a large saucepan over medium-high heat. Cook chicken and onion in oil 4 to 5 minutes, or until onion is tender. Stir in the chicken broth, green chiles, garlic powder, cumin, oregano, cilantro, and cayenne pepper. Reduce heat, and simmer for 15 minutes. Stir in the beans, and simmer for 5 more minutes, or until chicken is no longer pink and juices run clear. Garnish with green onion and shredded cheese.

Award Winning Chili

Ingredients	Directions
❖ 1 (14.5 ounce) can stewed tomatoes, chopped ❖ 1 (6 ounce) can tomato paste ❖ 1 carrot, sliced ❖ 1 onion, chopped ❖ 2 stalks celery, chopped ❖ 1/4 cup white wine ❖ 1 pinch crushed red pepper flakes ❖ 1/4 cup chopped green bell ❖ pepper ❖ 1/4 cup chopped red bell pepper 1/3 cup bottled steak sauce ❖ 5 slices bacon ❖ 1 1/2 pounds ground beef ❖ 1 (1.25 ounce) package chili seasoning mix ❖ 1 teaspoon ground cumin ❖ 1 (15 ounce) can kidney beans, drained ❖ 1 tablespoon chopped fresh cilantro ❖ 1 tablespoon chopped fresh parsley	In a large pot over medium-low heat, combine tomatoes, tomato paste, carrot, onion, celery, wine, pepper flakes, bell peppers and steak sauce. While tomato mixture is simmering, in a large skillet over medium heat, cook bacon until crisp. Remove to paper towels. Cook beef in bacon drippings until brown; drain. Stir chili seasoning into ground beef. Stir seasoned beef, cumin and bacon into tomato mixture. Continue to simmer until vegetables are tender and flavors are well blended. Stir in beans, cilantro and parsley. Heat through and serve.

Ez's Slow Cooker Hot Chili

Ingredients	Directions
❖ 1 onion, chopped ❖ 1 green bell pepper, chopped ❖ 1 clove garlic, minced ❖ 2 tablespoons olive oil ❖ 2 pounds ground beef ❖ 4 (11.5 ounce) cans tomato-vegetable juice cocktail ❖ 1 (10.75 ounce) can condensed tomato soup ❖ 1 (16 ounce) can chili beans,	In a large skillet over medium heat, saute the onion, green bell pepper and garlic in the oil for 5 minutes, or until tender. Stir in the beef and cook until brown. Transfer these ingredients to a slow cooker. Then, to the slow cooker, add tomato-vegetable juice, soup, chili beans, cayenne pepper, chili powder, soy sauce and water.

drained	
❖ 1/8 teaspoon cayenne pepper	Cover slow cooker and cook on low setting for 2 hours.
❖ 3 tablespoons chili powder	
❖ 1 tablespoon soy sauce	
❖ 1 cup water	

Slow Cooker Bean Casserole AKA Sweet Chili

Ingredients	Directions
❖ 1/2 cup ketchup ❖ 1/4 cup molasses ❖ 1 teaspoon dry mustard ❖ 1 (16 ounce) can baked beans with pork ❖ 1 teaspoon salt ❖ 1/2 teaspoon ground black pepper ❖ 4 slices bacon ❖ 1 large green bell pepper, chopped ❖ 1 1/2 pounds ground beef	In a slow cooker, mix together ketchup, molasses, mustard, pork and beans, salt, and pepper. Cook bacon and bell pepper in a large skillet over medium heat for about 5 to 7 minutes, then add to the slow cooker. In same skillet, brown beef, and stir into the slow cooker. Cover, and cook on High setting for 1 hour.

Easy Chili III

Ingredients	Directions
❖ 3 pounds ground beef ❖ 1 large onion, chopped ❖ 1 medium head garlic, peeled and chopped ❖ 1 cup dry black beans ❖ 1 cup dry kidney beans ❖ 1 cup dry pinto beans ❖ 2 (28 ounce) cans diced tomatoes, drained ❖ 3 cups tomato paste ❖ 1 (8 ounce) can tomato sauce ❖ 2 tablespoons chili powder, or to	In a large pot over medium heat, cook beef, onion and garlic until meat is brown. Stir in black beans, kidney beans, pinto beans, tomatoes, tomato paste and tomato sauce. Season with chili powder, salt, pepper and pepper sauce. Reduce heat, cover and simmer 2 to 3 hours, until beans are tender.

taste ❖ 1 teaspoon hot pepper sauce, or to taste ❖ salt and pepper to taste	

Debdoozie's Blue Ribbon Chili

Ingredients	Directions
❖ 2 pounds ground beef ❖ 1/2 onion, chopped ❖ 1 teaspoon ground black pepper ❖ 1/2 teaspoon garlic salt ❖ 2 1/2 cups tomato sauce ❖ 1 (8 ounce) jar salsa ❖ 4 tablespoons chili seasoning mix ❖ 1 (15 ounce) can light red kidney beans ❖ 1 (15 ounce) can dark red kidney beans	In a large saucepan over medium heat, combine the ground beef and the onion and saute for 10 minutes, or until meat is browned and onion is tender. Drain grease, if desired. Add the ground black pepper, garlic salt, tomato sauce, salsa, chili seasoning mix and kidney beans. Mix well, reduce heat to low and simmer for at least an hour.

Chili II

Ingredients	Directions
❖ 2 pounds ground beef ❖ 1 onion, chopped ❖ 2 (16 ounce) cans chili beans ❖ 1 (15 ounce) can tomato sauce ❖ 1 (10 ounce) can diced tomatoes with green chile peppers ❖ 1 (14.5 ounce) can peeled and diced tomatoes ❖ 11 1/2 fluid ounces tomato juice ❖ 1 (4 ounce) can diced green chiles ❖ 1 (1.25 ounce) package chili seasoning mix	Cook ground beef and onion until done. In slow cooker or Dutch oven add all ingredients together. Simmer several hours.

Black Bean Chili

Ingredients	Directions
❖ 1 1/2 pounds boneless pork, cut into 1/2-inch cubes ❖ 2 (15.5 ounce) cans black beans, drained ❖ 1 cup chopped onion ❖ 1 cup chopped yellow bell pepper ❖ 1 cup thick and chunky salsa ❖ 1 (15 ounce) can canned diced tomatoes ❖ 2 cloves garlic, minced ❖ 1 teaspoon chili powder ❖ 1/2 teaspoon cumin ❖ 1/4 teaspoon crushed red pepper Garnish: sour cream, shredded Cheddar cheese (optional)	Combine all ingredients except garnishes in 3 1/2-quart slow cooker. Cover and cook on low heat setting 7 to 8 hours. Top individual bowls with sour cream and Cheddar cheese.

Green Chili Stew

Ingredients	Directions
❖ 1 1/2 pounds boneless pork loin roast, cut into 3/4-inch cubes ❖ 2 tablespoons olive or canola oil ❖ 1 large onion, diced ❖ 1 jalapeno pepper, seeded and chopped* ❖ 3 garlic cloves, minced ❖ 1 1/2 teaspoons ground cumin ❖ 1 teaspoon salt ❖ 1/4 teaspoon white pepper ❖ 1 bay leaf ❖ 5 medium potatoes, peeled and cubed ❖ 3 cups water ❖ 1 (14.5 ounce) can diced tomatoes, undrained ❖ 3 (4 ounce) cans chopped green chilies	In a Dutch oven or large saucepan, brown pork in oil. Add the onion, jalapenos, garlic, cumin, salt, pepper and bay leaf; saute until onion is tender. Add potatoes and water; bring to boil. Reduce heat; cover and simmer for 15-20 minutes or until potatoes are tender. Add tomatoes and chilies; simmer 10 minutes longer. Discard bay leaf before serving.

Texas Style Chili with Spicy Jalapeno Chicken

Ingredients	Directions
❖ 2 (12 ounce) packages al ❖ frescoB® Spicy Jalapeno Chicken Sausage ❖ 2 tablespoons olive oil ❖ 1/2 cup chopped onion ❖ 1 green pepper, chopped ❖ 1 red pepper, chopped ❖ 1 yellow pepper, chopped ❖ 3 cloves garlic ❖ 2 (15 ounce) cans black soy beans ❖ 3 tablespoons chili powder (spicy) ❖ 1 teaspoon ground cumin ❖ 1 teaspoon dried oregano ❖ 2 bay leaves	Slice al fresco chicken sausage and saute with oil, onions, peppers, and garlic. Add remaining ingredients and stir well. Cook on low for about 1 hour, stirring occasionally.

Fruity Chili

Ingredients	Directions
❖ 2 (14 ounce) cans tomato sauce ❖ 2 (15 ounce) cans kidney beans, rinsed and drained ❖ 2 tablespoons chili powder ❖ 1 tablespoon white sugar ❖ 1 pinch cayenne pepper (optional) ❖ 1 pound ground beef ❖ 2 tablespoons chili powder ❖ 1 tablespoon white sugar ❖ 1 pinch cayenne pepper (optional) ❖ 1 teaspoon cooking oil ❖ 1/2 red onion, chopped ❖ 1 banana pepper, chopped ❖ 1 apple - peeled, cored, and chopped ❖ 1 peach - peeled, pitted, and chopped	Combine the tomato sauce, kidney beans, 2 tablespoons chili powder, 1 tablespoon sugar, and cayenne pepper in a large sauce pan; bring to a simmer over low heat. Place a large skillet over medium-high heat; place the ground beef in the skillet; season with 2 tablespoons chili powder, 1 tablespoon sugar, and the cayenne pepper; cook until brown; add to the sauce mixture. Heat the oil in a small skillet over medium-high heat; cook the onion in the oil until slightly browned; add to the sauce mixture, along with the apple, peach, and banana pepper. Allow to simmer another 1 to 2 minutes until hot.

Bry's Chocolate Lamb Chili

Ingredients	Directions
❖ 1 medium onion, chopped ❖ 1 pound lean ground lamb ❖ 2 tablespoons olive oil ❖ 1/2 teaspoon red pepper flakes ❖ 1/2 tablespoon dried basil ❖ 1 teaspoon cumin ❖ 1/8 teaspoon cinnamon ❖ 2 large cloves garlic, minced ❖ 3 1/2 tablespoons chili powder ❖ 1/2 teaspoon dried oregano ❖ 1 teaspoon unsweetened cocoa powder ❖ 1 teaspoon white sugar ❖ 1 bay leaf ❖ salt and pepper to taste ❖ 1 (14.5 ounce) can diced tomatoes with juice ❖ 4 cups red beans, with liquid	In a large pot, cook onions and ground lamb in olive oil over medium heat. When onions are soft and meat browned, season with red pepper flakes, basil, cumin, cinnamon, garlic, chili powder, dried oregano, cocoa powder, sugar, and bay leaf, and salt and pepper to taste. Cook for 1 or 2 minutes. Stir in tomatoes and beans. Increase heat to bring soup to a boil. Reduce heat, and simmer for 15 minutes.

Chili Cheese Dip

Ingredients	Directions
❖ 1 pound process American cheese, cubed ❖ 1 (15 ounce) can chili con carne without beans ❖ 1 (4 ounce) can chopped green chilies ❖ Tortilla chips	Combine cheese, chili and chilies in a saucepan or fondue pot. Heat over medium-low, stirring frequently, until the cheese melts. Serve warm with tortilla chips.

Mean Old Chili

Ingredients	Directions
❖ 1/4 cup Worcestershire sauce ❖ 1 clove garlic, chopped ❖ 2 tablespoons red pepper flakes ❖ 1 teaspoon distilled white vinegar ❖ 1 teaspoon dried oregano ❖ 1 teaspoon dried basil ❖ 1 teaspoon black pepper ❖ 2 tablespoons olive oil ❖ 1 tablespoon chili powder, or to taste ❖ 2 1/2 pounds beef chuck roast, cubed ❖ 1/2 pound fresh hot chilies, cut crosswise into thirds ❖ 2 cups chopped fresh tomato ❖ 1 red bell pepper, cut into 1 inch pieces ❖ 1 (15.5 ounce) can pinto beans, drained ❖ 1 teaspoon red pepper flakes, or to taste	In a glass baking pan, stir together the Worcestershire sauce, garlic, 2 tablespoons red pepper flakes, vinegar, oregano, basil, black pepper and olive oil. Place the meat into the sauce; cover and marinate overnight in the refrigerator. Preheat an outdoor grill for medium-high heat. Remove meat from the marinade, and discard marinade. Thread the marinated beef, chili peppers, and red bell pepper onto skewers. Grill the skewers about 4 to 6 minutes on each side, or until the meat is of the desired doneness. Place a large saucepan or Dutch oven over medium heat. Remove meat and peppers from skewers, and place them in the pan. Season with chili powder, and stir in tomatoes and pinto beans. Sprinkle in the remaining red pepper flakes.

Grilled Prawns with Garlic-Chili Sauce

Ingredients	Directions
❖ 1 pound jumbo prawns ❖ 2 tablespoons cooking oil ❖ 2 tablespoons minced garlic ❖ 2 tablespoons thinly sliced lemon grass ❖ 5 fresh Thai chile peppers, sliced thin ❖ 1 shallot, sliced thin ❖ 2 kaffir lime leaves ❖ 1 tablespoon fish sauce, or to	Preheat an outdoor grill for medium heat; lightly oil the grate. Cook the shrimp on the hot grill until they are bright pink on the outside and the meat is no longer transparent in the center, 5 to 10 minutes. Arrange the prawns on a serving platter. Heat the oil in a skillet over medium heat.

taste ❖ 1 lime, juiced ❖ 1 tablespoon Thai roasted chilli paste (nam prik pao) ❖ 1 tablespoon torn fresh mint leaves	Fry the garlic in the hot oil until brown, 7 to 10 minutes. Remove from heat and stir the lemon grass, chile peppers, shallot, lime leaves, fish sauce, lime juice, and chilli paste into the garlic; toss to combine. Spoon the sauce over the prawns. Garnish with the mint to serve.

Peoria Chili

Ingredients	Directions
❖ 2 pounds ground beef ❖ 1 medium onion, chopped ❖ 1 (28 ounce) can diced tomatoes, with liquid ❖ 1 (46 ounce) can tomato juice ❖ 1 tablespoon chili powder ❖ 1 tablespoon sugar ❖ salt and pepper to taste ❖ 2 (15 ounce) cans red kidney beans, rinsed and drained Shredded Cheddar cheese	In a large kettle or Dutch oven, brown beef and onion. Drain off fat; add all remaining ingredients except beans and cheese. Cover and simmer 2-3 hours. Adjust seasonings, if necessary. Stir in beans and heat through. Before serving, top with shredded cheddar cheese, if desired.

Shay's Irish Chili

Ingredients	Directions
❖ 2 tablespoons vegetable oil ❖ 1 pound ground beef chuck ❖ 1 clove garlic, minced ❖ 1 large onion, chopped salt and pepper to taste ❖ 1 pinch ground nutmeg ❖ 2 teaspoons beef bouillon ❖ 1 tablespoon chili powder ❖ 1 tablespoon white sugar ❖ 1 (28 ounce) can diced tomatoes, drained ❖ 1/2 (19 ounce) can light red kidney	Heat the oil in a soup pot set over medium heat. Add the ground beef, garlic, and onion. Cook, stirring to crumble the ground beef, until beef is no longer pink. Drain off any excess grease. Season with salt, pepper, nutmeg, beef bouillon, and chili powder. Add the sugar, tomatoes, light and dark kidney beans and potatoes. Cover and simmer over medium-low heat for 1 hour, stirring occasionally.

beans, drained and mashed ❖ 1 (15.5 ounce) can dark red kidney beans, drained and rinsed ❖ 1 (15 ounce) can sliced potatoes, drained	

Texas Chili Beef Slices

Ingredients	Directions
❖ 2 pounds round steak ❖ 1 teaspoon meat tenderizer ❖ 1 onion, chopped ❖ 2 cloves garlic, minced ❖ 2 tablespoons distilled white vinegar ❖ 2 tablespoons vegetable oil ❖ 2 tablespoons Worcestershire sauce ❖ 2 teaspoons chili powder ❖ 1 (8 ounce) can tomato sauce ❖ 1 lemon, sliced ❖ 2 tablespoons brown sugar ❖ 1/2 teaspoon mustard powder ❖ 1/4 teaspoon hot pepper sauce	Sprinkle meat with meat tenderizer. Place in a shallow glass baking dish large enough to accommodate the meat. Mix together onion, garlic, vinegar, oil, Worcestershire sauce, and chili powder, and pour over steak. Marinate for 2 or more hours in the refrigerator. Preheat grill for medium-low heat. Brush grate with oil. Transfer steak to grill, reserving marinade. Cook, covered, for 30 to 40 minutes, or to your desired degree of doneness, turning once. Allow steak to rest for a few minutes off the heat. While meat is cooking prepare sauce. Combine reserved marinade, tomato sauce, lemon slices, brown sugar, mustard powder, and hot sauce in a medium saucepan. Simmer for 10 minutes over medium low heat. Slice meat across the grain. Spoon sauce over steak, and serve.

Touchdown Chili

Ingredients	Directions
❖ 2 pounds ground beef ❖ 1 large onion, chopped ❖ 6 cloves garlic, chopped ❖ 1/3 cup chili powder ❖ 1 1/2 teaspoons ground cumin ❖ 1 1/2 teaspoons dried basil ❖ 1 (28 ounce) can diced tomatoes with juice ❖ 1 (4 ounce) can diced green chile peppers, drained ❖ 1 (15 ounce) can tomato sauce ❖ 1 (12 fluid ounce) can or bottle beer ❖ 1 tablespoon white vinegar ❖ 3 tablespoons brown sugar ❖ 1 teaspoon hot pepper sauce (e.g. Tabascoв„ў) ❖ 2 teaspoons salt ❖ 1/2 teaspoon ground black pepper	Place the ground beef, onion and garlic in a large saucepan over medium heat. Cook, stirring to crumble the beef, until the beef is no longer pink and the onion is tender. Drain off the fat and return the pan to the stove. Combine the chili powder, cumin and basil; sprinkle over the beef. Cook and stir to coat the meat and toast the spices a little. Pour in the tomatoes, green chilies, tomato sauce, beer and vinegar. Bring to a boil and stir to loosen any bits that are stuck to the bottom of the pan. Mix in the brown sugar, hot pepper sauce, salt and pepper. Reduce the heat to low, cover and simmer for 3 hours. Remove the lid for the last 30 minutes of cooking.

Slow-Cooked Chili

Ingredients	Directions
❖ 2 pounds ground beef ❖ 2 (16 ounce) cans kidney beans, rinsed and drained ❖ 2 (14.5 ounce) cans diced tomatoes, undrained ❖ 1 (8 ounce) can tomato sauce ❖ 2 medium onions, chopped ❖ 1 green pepper, chopped ❖ 2 cloves garlic, minced ❖ 2 tablespoons chili powder ❖ 2 teaspoons salt ❖ 1 teaspoon pepper Shredded Cheddar cheese	In a skillet, cook beef over medium heat until no longer pink; drain. Transfer to a slow cooker. Add the next nine ingredients. Cover and cook on low for 8-10 hours or on high for 4 hours. Garnish individual servings with cheese if desired.

Italian Style Chili

Ingredients	Directions
❖ 1 pound lean ground beef ❖ 3/4 cup chopped onion ❖ 1 (26 ounce) jar three cheese spaghetti sauce ❖ 1 1/2 cups water ❖ 2 teaspoons sugar ❖ 1 (14.5 ounce) can diced tomatoes ❖ 1 (4 ounce) can sliced mushrooms ❖ 2 ounces sliced pepperoni ❖ 1 tablespoon beef bouillon ❖ 1 tablespoon chili powder ❖ 1 (14.5 ounce) can kidney beans, drained and rinsed ❖ 1 cup shredded Cheddar cheese	Crumble ground beef into a large stock pot over medium-high heat. Add onions, and cook, stirring, until beef is evenly browned. Drain grease, if necessary. Pour in the spaghetti sauce, water, sugar, tomatoes, mushrooms, pepperoni, bouillon, chili powder and kidney beans. Bring to a boil. Reduce heat, and simmer uncovered for 30 minutes, stirring occasionally, to blend flavors.

Jill's Vegetable Chili

Ingredients	Directions
❖ 1 pound cubed turkey breast ❖ 1 cup minced onion ❖ 1 tablespoon minced garlic ❖ 2 teaspoons chili powder ❖ 1/2 teaspoon ground cumin ❖ 1/8 teaspoon ground cinnamon ❖ 1 (14.5 ounce) can peeled and diced tomatoes ❖ 1 (14 ounce) can chicken broth ❖ 1 (15 ounce) can kidney beans ❖ 1 (15 ounce) can pinto beans ❖ 1 (10 ounce) package frozen corn kernels	In a large pot over medium heat, cook turkey until browned. Stir in onions, cover and cook 5 minutes. Stir in garlic, chili powder, cumin and cinnamon and cook until fragrant, about a minute. Pour in tomatoes and bring to a boil. Stir in broth, kidney beans, pinto beans and corn and bring to a boil again. Then reduce heat and simmer 10 minutes, or until thoroughly heated.

Cheesy Chili Dip I

Ingredients	Directions
❖ 1/2 pound finely chopped pork ❖ 16 ounces processed cheese food, cubed ❖ 1 (10 ounce) can diced tomatoes with green chile peppers, drained ❖ 1 cup condensed cream of mushroom soup ❖ 1 (15 ounce) can chili ❖ 1 (14.5 ounce) package tortilla chips	Place pork in a medium skillet. Cook over medium heat until evenly brown. Drain and set aside. In a crockpot or slow cooker over medium heat, combine the processed cheese food, diced tomatoes with green chile peppers, cream of mushroom soup, chili and cooked pork. Heat until all the cheese is melted. Serve with tortilla chips.

Lightning Source UK Ltd.
Milton Keynes UK
UKHW051047100621
385265UK00004B/26